Lecture Notes in Computer Science 1182

Edited by G. Goos, J. Hartmanis and J. van Leeuwen

Advisory Board: W. Brauer D. Gries J. Stoer

Springer
Berlin
Heidelberg
New York
Barcelona
Budapest
Hong Kong
London
Milan
Paris
Santa Clara
Singapore
Tokyo

Waqar Hasan

Optimization
of SQL Queries
for Parallel Machines

 Springer

Series Editors

Gerhard Goos, Karlsruhe University, Germany

Juris Hartmanis, Cornell University, NY, USA

Jan van Leeuwen, Utrecht University, The Netherlands

Author

Waqar Hasan
Stanford University, Department of Computer Science
Stanford, CA 94305, USA
E-mail: hasan@db.stanford.edu

Cataloging-in-Publication data applied for

Die Deutsche Bibliothek - CIP-Einheitsaufnahme

Hasan, Waqar:
Optimization of SQL queries for parallel machines / Waqar
Hasan. - Berlin ; Heidelberg ; New York ; Barcelona ;
Budapest ; Hong Kong ; London ; Milan ; Paris ; Santa Clara ;
Singapore ; Tokyo : Springer, 1996
  (Lecture notes in computer science ; 1182)
  Zugl.: Stanford, CA, Univ., Diss.
  ISBN 3-540-62065-6
NE: GT

CR Subject Classification (1991): H.2, H.3, E.5

ISSN 0302-9743
ISBN 3-540-62065-6 Springer-Verlag Berlin Heidelberg New York

© Springer-Verlag Berlin Heidelberg 1996
Printed in Germany

Typesetting: Camera-ready by author
SPIN 10550447   06/3142 – 5 4 3 2 1 0   Printed on acid-free paper

To my father

Dr. Amir Hasan

for showing me the paths that I follow.

Foreword

Performance in computing, and particularly in data access, is crucial as our dependence on computing becomes pervasive. Continued innovation is essential for increases in performance to keep up with our requirements: at any time in the past there has been a majority of tasks which can be performed in time, while there has been a remainder, the tail of the distribution, that provides a challenge. In addition, we are always facing some problems that are in the infeasible range.

As examples for the three classes of problems, namely satisfactory, challenging, and infeasible, we see in the arena of information processing, respectively, routine business processing, delivering information for decision-making from distributed large databases, and prediction of future events from models and historical data.

Performance in a computing system is improved in two dimensions: using higher speed in the individual modules and increasing the number of modules that can operate in parallel. These two dimensions are not independent, since the coordination and communication required in parallel execution increases the amount of work to be done by each module. Crucial in this balance is hence the granularity, the size of the modules. At the very fine grain the tradeoffs are well understood. Computer architectures, in various generations, have moved from say 8-bit, to 16-bit, 32-bit, and even wider paths. There is, however, a diminishing return here: if the natural data elements are small, and interact to inhibit parallel operation, then wider data paths do not provide an advantage.

Databases deal with mixed granularity. The primitive elemental values being stored are often small, but are aggregated into records of hundreds of elements, and then stored in files or tables containing thousands or millions of records. Relevant data for even a modest problem may be found on dozens of computers distributed anywhere over world-wide networks.

This monograph provides both insights and algorithms pertaining to parallel operation at a practical granularity relevant to database system operations. Tables or object classes provide sizable objects that can be treated in parallel while permitting serial, pipelined overlap. Modules can also be cloned by partitioning and replicating data objects. These approaches interact with each other as well, making the selection of effective processing schedules yet more complex. Fortunately, the algebras over these objects are well-behaved, so that their operations can be completely and precisely defined.

This work provides an approach that balances the advantages and costs of parallel execution. Module granularity is determined by the actual operations being scheduled while respecting intrinsic limits on available parallelism such as timing and data-placement constraints and accounting for the trade-off between using parallel execution and incurring communication costs. The result is applicable to modern system configurations, where computation is performed on pipelining-capable workstations operating in parallel. Further research will have to focus on dynamic aspects of parallel computation, letting the scheduling itself overlap with the computation, since this work seems to be able to exploit all the information likely to be available prior to execution in practical systems.

Stanford, California, USA   *Gio Wiederhold*
September 1996

Preface

This book is about optimization techniques to determine the best way of exploiting parallel execution for SQL queries against large databases. It is the published version of my PhD dissertation at Stanford University. The techniques in this book are useful in the construction of SQL compilers that can exploit parallel machines effectively.

SQL permits questions to be posed declaratively. Users are insulated from the physical hardware and the layout of the data and thus are able to avoid the complex procedural details of programming a parallel machine. A Data Base Management System (DBMS) answers a SQL query by first finding a procedural plan to execute the query and subsequently executing the plan to produce the query result. This book provides techniques for the problem of *parallel query optimization*: Given a SQL query, find the parallel plan that delivers the query result in minimal time.

I express my gratitude to the people and organizations that made my thesis possible. Gio Wiederhold was a constant source of intellectual support. He encouraged me to learn and use a variety of techniques from different areas of Computer Science. Rajeev Motwani helped enhance my understanding of theory and contributed significantly to the ideas in my thesis. Jeff Ullman was a source of useful discussions and I thank him for his helpful and incisive comments. Ravi Krishnamurthy served as a mentor and a source of interesting ideas and challenging questions. Hector Garcia-Molina provided helpful advice. Jim Gray helped me understand the realities of parallel query processing.

My thesis topic grew out of work at Hewlett-Packard Laboratories and was supported by a fellowship from Hewlett-Packard. I express my gratitude to Hewlett-Packard Company and thank my managers Umesh Dayal, Dan Fishman, Peter Lyngbaek, and Marie-Anne Neimat for management and intellectual and moral support.

I thank Tandem Computers for providing access to a parallel machine, the NonStop SQL/MP parallel DBMS, and for permitting publication of experimental results. I am grateful to Susanne Englert, Ray Glasstone, and Shyam Johari for making this possible and for helping me understand Tandem systems.

The following friends and colleagues were a source of invaluable discussions and diversions: Sang Cha, Surajit Chaudhuri, Philippe DeSmedt, Mike Heytens, Curt Kolovson, Stephanie Leichner, Sheralyn Listgarten, Arif Merchant, Inderpal Mumick, Pandu Nayak, Peter Rathmann, Donovan Schneider, Arun Swami, Kevin Wilkinson, Xiaolei Qian.

My thesis would not have been possible without the support and understanding of my family. I thank my father, Dr. Amir Hasan, for providing the inspiration to pursue a PhD. I thank my mother, Fatima Hasan, my brothers Safdar, Javed, and Zulfiquar, and sister Seemin for their love and encouragement. I owe a debt to my wife Shirin and son Arif for putting up with the long hours that made this work possible.

Stanford, California, USA   *Waqar Hasan*
September 1996

Abstract

Parallel execution offers a solution to the problem of reducing the response time of SQL queries against large databases. As a declarative language, SQL allows users to avoid the complex procedural details of programming a parallel machine. A DBMS answers a SQL query by first finding a procedural plan to execute the query and subsequently executing the plan to produce the query result. We address the problem of *parallel query optimization*: Given a SQL query, find the parallel plan that delivers the query result in minimal time.

We develop optimization algorithms using models that incorporate the sources of parallelism as well as obstacles to achieving speedup. One obstacle is inherent limits on available parallelism due to parallel and precedence constraints between operators and due to data placement constraints that essentially pre-allocate some subset of operators. Another obstacle is that the overhead of exploiting parallelism may increase total work thus reducing or even offsetting the benefit of parallel execution. Our experiments with Non-Stop SQL, a commercial parallel DBMS, show communication of data across processors to be a significant source of increase in work.

We adopt a two-phase approach to parallel query optimization: *join ordering and query rewrite* (JOQR), followed by *parallelization*. The JOQR phase minimizes the total work to compute a query. The parallelization phase extracts parallelism and schedules resources to minimize response time. We make contributions to both phases. Our work is applicable to queries that include operations such as grouping, aggregation, foreign functions, and set intersection and difference, and joins.

We develop algorithms for the JOQR phase that minimize total cost while accounting for the communication cost of repartitioning data. Using a model that abstracts physical characteristics of data, such as partitioning, as colors, we devise tree coloring algorithms that are efficient and guarantee optimality.

We model the parallelization phase as scheduling a tree of inter-dependent operators with computation and communication costs represented as node and edge weights. Scheduling a weighted operator tree on a parallel machine poses a class of novel multi-processor scheduling problems that differ from the classical in several ways.

We develop and compare several efficient algorithms for the problem of scheduling a pipelined operator tree in which all operators run in parallel using inter-operator parallelism. Given the NP-hardness of the problem, we assess the quality of our algorithms by measuring their performance ratio which is the ratio of the response time of the generated schedule to that of the optimal. We prove worst-case bounds on the performance ratios of our algorithms and measure the average cases using simulation.

We address the problem of scheduling a pipelined operator tree using both pipelined and partitioned parallelism. We characterize optimal schedules and investigate two classes of schedules that we term symmetric and balanced.

The results in this thesis enable the construction of SQL compilers that can exploit parallel machines effectively.

Table of Contents

1. **Introduction** 1
    1.1 Minimizing Response Time: Sources and Deterrents 1
        1.1.1 Sources of Speedup 2
        1.1.2 Deterrents to Speedup 3
    1.2 Model for Parallel Query Optimization 4
        1.2.1 Annotated Query Trees 5
        1.2.2 Operator Trees 5
        1.2.3 Parallel Machine Model 7
    1.3 Organization of Thesis 8
    1.4 Related Work 9
        1.4.1 Query Optimization for Centralized Databases 9
        1.4.2 Query Optimization for Distributed Databases 9
        1.4.3 Query Optimization for Parallel Databases 10

2. **Price of Parallelism** 13
    2.1 Introduction 13
    2.2 Tandem Architecture: An Overview 14
        2.2.1 Parallel and Fault-Tolerant Hardware 14
        2.2.2 Message Based Software 16
        2.2.3 Performance Characteristics 16
    2.3 Parallelism in NonStop SQL/MP 17
        2.3.1 Use of Intra-operator Parallelism 17
        2.3.2 Process Structure 18
    2.4 Startup Costs 20
    2.5 Costs of Operators and Communication 20
        2.5.1 Experimental Setup 22
        2.5.2 Costs of Scans, Predicates and Aggregation 23
        2.5.3 Costs of Local and Remote Communication 24
        2.5.4 Cost of Repartitioned Communication 26
        2.5.5 Costs of Join Operators 27
        2.5.6 Costs of Grouping Operators 30
    2.6 Parallel Versus Sequential Execution 31
        2.6.1 Parallelism Can Reduce Work 31
        2.6.2 Parallelism Can Increase Response Time 33

2.7 Summary of Findings 33

3. **JOQR Optimizations** 35
   3.1 A Model for Minimizing Communication 36
       3.1.1 Partitioning 36
       3.1.2 Repartitioning Cost 38
       3.1.3 Optimization Problem 38
   3.2 Algorithms for Query Tree Coloring 39
       3.2.1 Problem Simplification 40
       3.2.2 A Greedy Algorithm for Distinct Pre-Colorings 42
       3.2.3 Algorithm for Repeated Colors 43
       3.2.4 Extensions: Using Sets of Colors 46
   3.3 Model for Methods and Physical Properties 48
       3.3.1 Annotated Query Trees and Their Cost 50
   3.4 Extension of ColorSplit for Methods and Physical Properties . 52
   3.5 Model with Join Ordering 53
       3.5.1 Join Ordering Without Physical Properties 54
       3.5.2 Join Ordering with Physical Properties 55
   3.6 Usage of Algorithms 56

4. **Scheduling Pipelined Parallelism** 59
   4.1 Problem Definition 59
   4.2 Identifying Worthless Parallelism 62
       4.2.1 Worthless Edges and Monotone Trees 63
       4.2.2 The GreedyChase Algorithm 65
       4.2.3 Lower Bounds 65
   4.3 The Modified LPT Algorithm 66
   4.4 Connected Schedules 68
       4.4.1 Connected Schedules When Communication is Free ... 68
       4.4.2 BalancedCuts with Communication Costs 73
   4.5 Connected Schedules as an Approximation 73
   4.6 Heuristics for POT Scheduling 77
       4.6.1 A Hybrid Algorithm 78
       4.6.2 The Greedy Pairing Algorithm 78
   4.7 Approximation Algorithms 79
       4.7.1 A Two-Stage Approach 80
       4.7.2 The LocalCuts Algorithm 82
       4.7.3 The BoundedCuts Algorithm 84
   4.8 Experimental Comparison 89
       4.8.1 Experimental Setup 90
       4.8.2 Experimental Comparison 90
       4.8.3 Performance of Hybrid 91
       4.8.4 Comparison of Hybrid, LocalCuts and BoundedCuts .. 91
       4.8.5 Behavior of Lower Bound 92
   4.9 Discussion 94

5. Scheduling Mixed Parallelism 95
   5.1 Problem Definition 95
   5.2 Balanced Schedules 99
   5.3 Symmetric Schedules.................................... 102
   5.4 Scheduling Trees with Two Nodes 111
   5.5 Discussion 112

6. Summary and Future Work 115
   6.1 Summary of Contributions.............................. 115
   6.2 Future Work 118

References 121

Index 131

List of Figures

1.1   Query Processing Architecture   2
1.2   Phases and Sub-phases of Parallel Query Optimization   4
1.3   (A) Annotated Query Tree (B) Corresponding Operator Tree   6

2.1   (A) Tandem Architecture (B) Abstraction as Shared-Nothing   15
2.2   Process Startup: With (Solid) and Without (Dotted) Process Reuse.   21
2.3   Local, Remote and Repartitioned Communication   21
2.4   Scan with 1 Predicate (Dotted), 2 Predicates (Solid), Aggregation
      (Dashed)   24
2.5   Scan and Aggregation   25
2.6   Process Structure: (A) No Communication (B) Local (C) Remote.   26
2.7   Local and Repartitioned Execution   28
2.8   Local (Dotted) and Repartitioned (Solid) Communication   29
2.9   Query Using Simple-Hash (Dashed), Sort-Merge (Solid) and Nested
      Join (Dotted)   29
2.10 Hash (Solid) and Sort (Dotted) Grouping Costs   30
2.11 Process Structure: Sequential and Parallel Execution   32

3.1   Query Trees: Hatched Edges Show Repartitioning   37
3.2   (i) Query Tree; (ii) Coloring of Cost 7; (iii) Minimal Coloring of
      Cost 6   40
3.3   (i) Split Colored Interior Node (ii) Collapse Uncolored Leaves   41
3.4   (i) Query Tree (ii) Suboptimal DLC Coloring (cost=9) (iii) Opti-
      mal Coloring (cost=8)   43
3.5   Problem Decomposition After Coloring Node i   44
3.6   Opt and Optc Tables for Tree of Figure 3.4   45
3.7   Interaction of Repartitioning with Join Predicates   48
3.8   Annotated Query Trees   49
3.9   Interaction of Repartitioning with Order of Joins   54
3.10 Decomposition of a Complex Query   57

4.1   A Pipelined Schedule and Its Execution   61
4.2   (A) Trace of *GreedyChase* (Worthless Edges Hatched) (B) Modi-
      fied LPT Schedule (C) Naive LPT Schedule   66
4.3   Example with Performance Ratio = n/p for *Modified LPT*   68

4.4   Connected Schedule as Cutting and Collapsing Edges   69
4.5   Fragments Formed by *BpSchedule* Before the Last Stage of *BalancedCuts*   73
4.6   Examples with $\frac{L_C}{L_{opt}} = 2 - \frac{1}{\lceil \frac{p+1}{2} \rceil}$ 75
4.7   Performance Ratio=3 for Star of 10 Nodes Scheduled on 5 Processors   77
4.8   Subtrees $T_m, T_{m'}, T_{m''}$ for Nodes m, m', m''   86
4.9 C_{opt}^m   86
4.10 Performance of Hybrid (Solid), BalancedFragments (Dotted) and Modified LPT (Dashed) on Wide Trees   91
4.11 Performance of Hybrid (Solid), BalancedFragments (Dotted) and Modified LPT (Dashed) on Narrow Trees   92
4.12 Comparison of Hybrid (Solid), LocalCuts (Dashed) and BoundedCuts (Dotted) on Narrow Trees   92
4.13 Comparison of Hybrid (Solid), LocalCuts (Dashed) and BoundedCuts (Dotted) on Wide Trees   93
4.14 Performance of Optimal (Dotted) and Hybrid (Solid)   93

5.1   Execution with Mixed Parallelism   97
5.2   Structure of (Strongly) Minimal Schedule 102
5.3   Matrices for $p = 3$ 107
5.4   Counter-Example: Tree for Which Symmetric Schedule is a Saddle Point 110
5.5   Plot of $z = a_{11} + a_{21} - 2a_{11}a_{21}$ with a_{11} on x-Axis, a_{21} on y-Axis . 111
5.6   One Sided Schedule 113
5.7   Balanced Schedule for n=2 (Some Communication Arcs omitted) . 113

6.1   Phases and Sub-phases of Parallel Query Optimization 116

List of Tables

2.1   Parallelization Strategies and Join Methods   19
2.2   CPU Costs of Transfer and Computational Operations. (1K Tuples Occupy 1 Mbyte)   22

3.1   Examples of Input-Output Constraints   51

1. Introduction

Database systems provide competitive advantage to businesses by allowing quick determination of answers to business questions. Intensifying competition continues to increase the sizes of databases as well as the sophistication of queries against them. Parallel machines constructed from commodity hardware components offer higher performance as well as performance at a lower price as compared to sequential mainframes. Exploiting parallelism is therefore a natural solution for reducing the response times of queries against large databases [DG92, Val93].

SQL, the standard language for database access, is a declarative language. It insulates users from the complex procedural details of accessing and manipulating data. In particular, exploiting parallel machines does not require users to learn a new language or existing SQL code to be rewritten. Given a declarative query, the DBMS first devises a procedural plan and then executes the plan to produce the query result (see Figure 1.1). The problem of devising the *best* procedural plan for a SQL query is termed *query optimization.*

While the declarative nature of SQL allows users to benefit transparently from parallel machines, the DBMS must solve a new optimization problem. This new problem, termed *parallel query optimization*, is the subject of this thesis. It is defined as: Given an SQL query, find the parallel plan that delivers the query result with the least response time. The response time of a plan is the elapsed time between starting plan execution and delivering the query result.

1.1 Minimizing Response Time: Sources and Deterrents

In this thesis, we will exploit two complementary tactics for reducing the response time of a query (i.e. speeding up a query). Response time may be reduced by decreasing the total work to compute a query. It may also be reduced by partitioning work among multiple processors.

We will model two fundamental deterrents to achieving speedup through partitioning of work. First, there may be intrinsic limits on how work may be partitioned. The available parallelism may be such that it is impossible to partition work evenly among processors. Since response time is the time at which all processors have completed work, skewed processor loads reduce

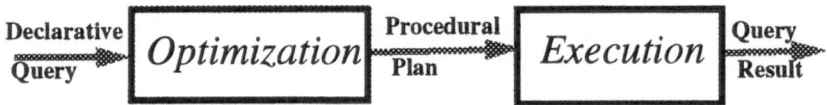

Fig. 1.1. Query Processing Architecture

speedup. As an extreme case, the available parallelism may be insufficient even to use all processors. The second deterrent is that partitioning may itself generate extra work. Thus, the overhead of exploiting parallelism may reduce, or even offset, the benefit from parallel execution.

1.1.1 Sources of Speedup

We first discuss tactics for reducing total work followed by tactics for partitioning work among multiple processors.

The total work to compute a query may be reduced by two tactics. First, algebraic laws may be applied to transform a query into an equivalent query by rearranging, replacing, or eliminating operators. If the equivalent query requires less work, we may compute it instead of the original query. Second, each operator (or collection of operators) has several alternative implementations each of which may be the best depending on the statistical and physical characteristics of the operands. Work may be reduced by choosing an appropriate combination of methods for each operator. While there has been substantial work on these tactics, parallel machines raise new aspects such as communication costs that require a fresh look at the problem.

The work in computing a query may be partitioned using three forms of parallelism: *independent, pipelined* and *partitioned.* Two operators neither of which uses data produced by the other may run simultaneously on distinct processors. Such inter-operator parallelism is termed independent parallelism. Since operators produce and consume sets of tuples, the tuples output by a producer can sometimes be fed to a consumer as they get produced. Such inter-operator concurrency is termed *pipelining* and, when the producer and consumer use distinct processors, is termed pipelined parallelism. A third form of parallelism, termed *partitioned* parallelism, provides intra-operator parallelism based on partitioning of data. We explain opportunities for partitioned parallelism for unary and binary operators below.

If $T = T_0 \cup T_1 \cup \ldots \cup T_k$ (where T, T_i are tables), then unary operators such as selection, projection, duplicate elimination, grouping and aggregation may be pushed through union using algebraic identities that essentially have the following form:

$$Op(T) = Op(T_0) \cup Op(T_1) \cup \ldots \cup Op(T_k)$$

The terms on the right hand side may be computed independently of each other, thus providing opportunity for parallel execution. The exact transformation is more complex for operators such as grouping and aggregation.

Binary operators such as equijoins, set intersection, and set subtraction may also exploit parallelism based on data partitioning. Consider the equijoin of tables T and S. Let $T = T_0 \cup T_1 \cup \ldots \cup T_k$ and $S = S_0 \cup S_1 \cup \ldots \cup S_k$ such that matching tuples go to matching partitions. In other words, if the value of the join column for tuple $t \in T$ matches the value of the join column for tuple $s \in S$ and, t goes to partition T_i then s must go to partition S_i. The following identity shows the opportunity for partitioned parallelism.

$$T \bowtie S = (T_1 \bowtie S_1) \cup (T_2 \bowtie S_2) \cup \ldots \cup (T_k \bowtie S_k) \qquad (1.1)$$

Similar identities apply to other binary operators. We also mention a related form of parallelism based on exploiting a combination of data replication and partitioning. It may be used for joins without requiring an equijoin predicate. The join operator may be parallelized by partitioning T and joining each partition with a replica of S. This strategy is termed *fragment and replicate* or *partition and replicate*. The transformation applies irrespective of the nature of the join predicate; specifically it also applies to Cartesian products.

$$T \bowtie S = (T_1 \bowtie S) \cup (T_2 \bowtie S) \cup \ldots \cup (T_k \bowtie S) \qquad (1.2)$$

1.1.2 Deterrents to Speedup

Speedup is limited by the intrinsic limits on *available parallelism* and by the *overheads* of exploiting parallelism.

Available parallelism is limited by several factors. Inter-operator parallelism is limited by timing constraints between operators. For example, a hash join works by first building a hash table on one operand and then probing the hash table for matches using tuples of the second operand. Since the hash table must be fully built before being probed, there is a *precedence* constraint in the computation. As another example, an operator that scans a table may pipe its output to the operator that builds a hash table. Such concurrency eliminates the need to buffer intermediate results. However, it places a *parallel* constraint in the computation. In many machine architectures, data on a specific disk may be accessed only by the processor that controls the disk. Thus *data placement* constraints limit both inter and intra-operator parallelism by localizing scan operations to specific processors. For example, if an Employee table is stored partitioned by department, a selection query that retrieves employees from a single department has no available parallelism.

Using parallel execution requires starting and initializing processes. These processes may then communicate substantial amounts of data. These *startup* and *communication* overheads increase total work. The increase is significant enough that careless use of parallelism can result in slowing down queries rather than speeding them up. The cost of communication is a function of the size of data communicated. While an individual operator may examine a relatively small portion of each tuple, all attributes that are used by any subsequent operator need to be communicated. Thus, communication costs can be an arbitrarily high portion of total cost.

1.2 Model for Parallel Query Optimization

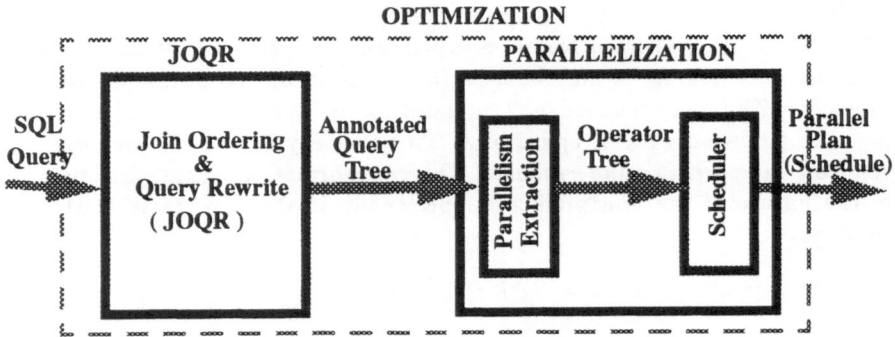

Fig. 1.2. Phases and Sub-phases of Parallel Query Optimization

We will use a two-phase approach to minimizing the response time of queries (Figure 1.2). The first phase applies the tactic of minimizing total work while the second applies the tactic of partitioning work among processors. The primary advantage of division into two phases is to reduce the conceptual complexity of parallel query optimization.

The first phase, JOQR (for Join Ordering and Query Rewrite, the two steps in a conventional optimizer [HFLP89]), produces an annotated query tree that fixes aspects such as the order of joins and the strategy for computing each join. While conventional query optimization deals with similar problems we will develop (in Chapter 3) models and algorithms that are cognizant of critical aspects of parallel execution. Thus rather than finding the best plan for sequential execution, our algorithms find the best plan while accounting for parallel execution.

The second phase, *parallelization*, converts the annotated query tree into a parallel plan. We break the parallelization phase into two steps, *parallelism extraction* followed by *scheduling*. Parallelism extraction produces an *operator tree* that identifies the atomic units of execution and their interdependence. It explicates the timing constraints among operators. We shall briefly discuss the extraction of parallelism in Section 1.2.2.

The scheduling step allocates machine resources to each operator. We shall develop models and algorithms for several scheduling problems in Chapters 4 and 5.

We observe that our two-phase approach differs from that adopted by Hong and Stonebraker [Hon92b]. We do not assume the first phase to be a conventional query optimizer. In fact, Chapter 3 shows how accounting for the communication overheads of parallel execution results in choices that differ from that made by a conventional optimizer.

1.2.1 Annotated Query Trees

A procedural plan for an SQL query is conventionally represented by an annotated query tree. Such trees encode procedural choices such as the order in which operators are evaluated and the method for computing each operator. Each tree node represents one (or several) relational operators. Annotations on the node represent the details of how it is to be executed. For example a join node may be annotated as being executed by a hash-join, and a base relation may be annotated as being accessed by an index-scan. The EXPLAIN statement of most SQL systems (such as NonStop SQL/MP [Tan94]) allows such trees to viewed by a user.

Example 1.2.1. The following SQL query retrieves the average of the salaries of all employees who are skilled in "Molding" and earn more than their managers. Figure 1.3(A) shows an annotated query tree for the query.
select avg(E.salary)
from Emp E, Emp M, EmpSkills S
where E.empNum = S.empNum **and** E.mgr = M.empNum **and**
        E.Salary > M.Salary **and** S.skill = "Molding"

1.2.2 Operator Trees

An *operator tree* exposes opportunities for parallelism by identifying the atomic units of execution and the timing constraints between them. Nodes of an operator tree are termed operators[1] and represent pieces of code that are deemed to be atomic. Edges represent the flow of data as well as timing constraints between these operators.

An operator takes zero or more input sets of tuples and produces a single output set. Operators are formed by appropriate factoring of the code that implements the relational operations specified in an annotated query tree. A

---

[1] The meaning of the term *operator* varies with the context. It is used to denote operators of the relational algebra, nodes of annotated query trees as well as nodes of operator trees. A query trees operator may consist of several relational operators. An operator tree operator is a piece of code that may not correspond to any relational or query tree operator.

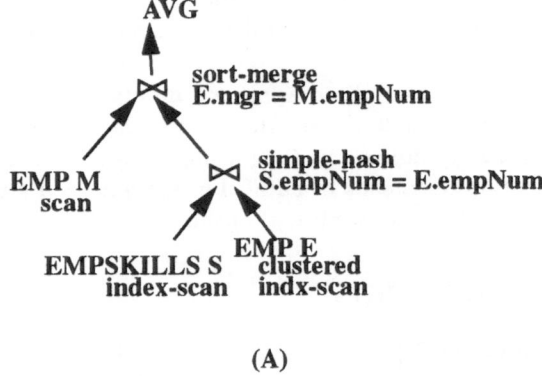

(A)

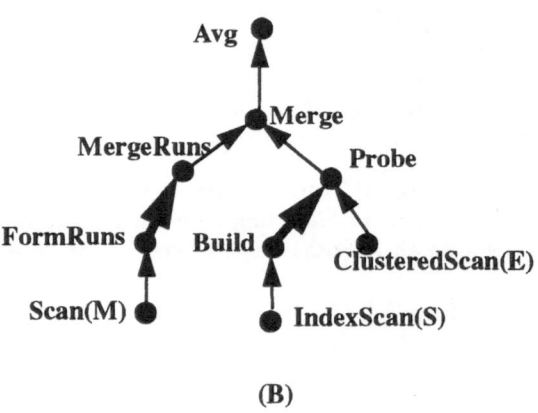

(B)

Fig. 1.3. (A) Annotated Query Tree (B) Corresponding Operator Tree

criteria in designing operators is to reduce inter-operator timing constraints to simple forms, i.e. parallel and precedence constraints.

The process of parallelism extraction is used to create operator trees from annotated query trees. This process may be viewed as applying a "macro-expansion" to each node of an annotated query tree. Since annotated query trees are constructed out of a fixed set of operators, the macro-expansion of each operator (of an annotated query tree) may be specified using mechanism such as rules. We will illustrate a sample expansion in Example 1.2.2.

Given an edge from operator i to j, a *parallel constraint* requires i and j to start at the same time and terminate at the same time. A *precedence constraint* requires j to start after i terminates. We define an edge that represents a parallel constraint to be a *pipelining* edge and an edge that represents a precedence constraint to be a *blocking* edge.

Parallel constraints capture pipelined execution. A pipeline between two operators is typically implemented using a flow control mechanism (such as a table queue [PMC+90]) to ensure that a fixed amount of memory suffices for the pipeline. Flow-control causes a fast producer to be slowed down by a slow consumer (or vice-versa) by stretching over a longer time period. Thus, the producer and consumer operators are constrained to run concurrently. Precedence constraints capture the behavior of operators that produce their output set only when they terminate. A consumer operator must wait for the producer to terminate before it may start execution.

Example 1.2.2. Figure 1.3(B) shows the operator tree for the annotated query tree of Figure 1.3(A). Thin edges are pipelining edges, thick edges are blocking. A simple hash join is broken into Build and Probe operators. Since a hash table must be fully built before it can be probed, the edge from Build to Probe is blocking. A sort-merge join sorts both inputs and then merges the sorted streams. The merging is implemented by the Merge operator. In this example, we assume the right input of sort-merge to be presorted. The operator tree shows the sort required for the left input broken into two operators FormRuns and MergeRuns. Since the merging of runs can start only after run formation, the edge from FormRuns to MergeRuns is blocking.

The operator tree exposes available parallelism. Partitioned parallelism may be used for any operator. Pipelined parallelism may be used for operators connected by pipelining edges. Two subtrees with no (transitive) precedence constraints between them may run independently. For example, the subtrees rooted at FormRuns and Build may run independently; operators FormRuns and Scan(M) may use pipelined parallelism; any operator may use partitioned parallelism.

1.2.3 Parallel Machine Model

We consider a parallel machine to consist of several identical nodes that communicate over an interconnect. The cost of a message consists of CPU cost incurred equally by both the sending and the receiving CPU. This cost is a function of the message size but independent of the identities of the sending and receiving CPUs (as long as they are distinct). In other words, we consider propagation delays and network topology to be irrelevant.

Propagation delay is the time delay for a single packet to travel over the interconnect. Query processing results in communicating large amounts of data over the interconnect. Such communication is typically achieved by sending a *stream* of packets – packets continue to be sent without waiting for already sent packets to reach the receiver. Thus, the propagation delay is independent of the number of packets and becomes insignificant when the number of packets is large.

Network topology is ignored for three reasons. First, it is unclear whether the behavior of sophisticated interconnects can be captured by simple topological models. Besides topological properties, interconnects also have embedded memory and specialized processors. Second, most architectures expect applications to regard the interconnect as a blackbox that has internal algorithms for managing messages. Third, there is tremendous variation in the topologies used for interconnects. Topology-dependent algorithms and software will be not be portable. Further, topology changes even in a specific machine as nodes fail and recover or are added or removed. Correctly and reliably adapting to such changes is complex. Incorporating topological knowledge in query processing and optimization will further complicate these tasks.

1.3 Organization of Thesis

In Chapter 2, we start with an experimental study that compares parallel and sequential execution in NonStop SQL/MP, a commercial parallel database system from Tandem Computers. The experiments establish communication to be a significant overhead in using parallel execution. They also show that startup costs may be made insignificant by modifying the execution system to reuse processes rather than creating them afresh.

In Chapter 3, we deal with models and algorithms for the JOQR phase. We pose minimizing communication as a tree coloring problem that is related to classical Multiway Cut problems. We then enhance the model to cover aspects such as the dependence of operator costs on physical properties of operands, the availability of multiple methods for an operator, and re-ordering of operators. The chapter also provide a clean abstraction of the basic ideas in the commercially popular System R algorithm.

In Chapter 3, we focus on the parallelization phase and consider the problem of managing pipelined parallelism. We start by developing the notion of worthless parallelism and showing how such parallelism may be eliminated. We then develop a variety of scheduling algorithms that assign operators to processors. We evaluate the algorithms by measuring their performance ratio which is the response time of the produced schedule divided by the response time of the optimal schedule. We establish bounds on the worst-case performance ratio by analytical methods and measure average-case performance ratios by experiments.

In Chapter 5, we consider the problem of scheduling a pipelined tree using both pipelined and partitioned parallelism. This is the continuous version of the discrete problem considered in the last chapter. We develop characterizations of optimal schedules and investigate two classes of schedules: symmetric and balanced.

Finally, in Chapter 6, we summarize our contributions and discuss some open problems.

1.4 Related Work

In this section, we discuss relevant past work in databases. The individual chapters will discuss related work from theory (Multiprocessor Scheduling [Gra69, Ull75], Multiway Cuts [DJP$^+$92] and Nonlinear optimization [GMW81, Lue89]) that we will find useful in developing optimization algorithms.

1.4.1 Query Optimization for Centralized Databases

Early work in query optimization followed two tracks. One was minimization of expression size [CM77, ASU79]. Expression size was measured by metrics, such as the number of joins in a query, that are independent of the database state. Another track was the development of heuristics based on models that considered the cost of an operator to depend on the size of its operands as well the data structures in which the operands were stored. For example, the cost of a join was estimated using the sizes of operands as well as whether an index to access an operand was available. Examples of such heuristics are performing selections and projections as early as possible [Hal76] and the Wong-Youseffi algorithm [WY76] for decomposing queries.

The System R project at IBM viewed the problem of selecting access paths and ordering join operators as an optimization problem with the objective of minimizing the total machine resource to compute a query [SAC$^+$79]. The estimation of machine resources was based on a cost model in which the cost of an operation depended on the statistical properties of operands (such as the minimum and maximum values in each column), the availability of indexes and the order in which tuples could be accessed. It also developed a combination of techniques to search for a good query plan. One of these techniques, the use of dynamic programming to speed up search, has been adopted by most commercial optimizers. Another technique, avoiding Cartesian products, is now recognized to produce bad plans for "star" queries (common in decision-support applications) in which a single large table is joined to several small tables.

System R also incorporated algebraic transformations that were applied as heuristics while parsing queries. The Starburst project recognized the growing importance of such heuristic transformations [Day87, Kin81, Kim82, GW87] by considering *Query Rewrite* to be a phase of optimization [PHH92].

The growing importance of decision-support has led to a rejuvenation of interest in discovering new transformations and algorithms to exploit the transformations [YL95, CS94, GHQ95, LMS94].

1.4.2 Query Optimization for Distributed Databases

While distributed and parallel databases are fundamentally similar, research in distributed query optimization was done in the early 1980s, a time at which communication over a network was prohibitively expensive and computer equipment was not cheap enough to be thrown at parallel processing.

The assumption of communication as the primary bottleneck led to the development of query execution techniques, notably semijoins [BC81], to reduce communication. Techniques for exploiting parallelism were largely ignored. For example, Apers et al. [AHY83] discuss independent parallelism but do not discuss either pipelined or partitioned parallelism. Thus, for historical reasons, the notion of distributed execution differs from parallel execution. Since the space of possible executions for a query is different, the optimization problems are different.

While Apers et al. considered minimizing response time as an optimization objective, most work, such as in SDD-1 [BGW+81] and R* [LMH+85, ML86], focused on minimizing resource consumption. SDD-1 assumed communication as the sole cost while R* considered local processing costs as well.

Techniques for distributing data using horizontal and vertical partitioning schemes [Ull89, CNW83, OV91] were developed for distributed data that also find a use in exploiting parallelism.

1.4.3 Query Optimization for Parallel Databases

Several research projects such as Bubba [BCC+90], Gamma [DGS+90], DBS3 [ZZBS93], and   Volcano [Gra90] devised techniques for placement of base tables and explored a variety of parallel execution techniques. This has yielded a well understood notion of parallel execution.

Considerable research has also been done on measuring the parallelism available in different classes of shapes for join trees. Schneider [Sch90] identified right-deep trees (with hash-join as the join method) as providing considerable parallelism. Chen et al. [CLYY92] investigated segmented right-deep trees and Ziane et al. [ZZBS93] investigated Zig-Zag trees. Such research focuses on evaluating a class of shapes rather than optimizing a single query. It may be used to subset the space of executions over which optimization should be performed.

Hong and Stonebraker [HS91] proposed the two-phase approach to parallel query optimization. They used a conventional query optimizer as the first phase. For parallelization, they considered exploiting partitioned and independent parallelism but not pipelined parallelism. While they ignored communication costs, we note that Hong [Hon92b] conjectured the XPRS approach to be inapplicable to architectures such as shared-nothing that have significant communication costs.

Hong [Hon92a] develops a parallelization algorithm to maximize machine utilization under restrictive assumptions. The parallel machine is assumed to consist of a single disk (RAID) and multiple processors and each operator is assumed to have CPU and IO requirements. Assuming that two operators, one CPU-bound and the other IO-bound to always be available for simultaneous execution, the algorithm computes the degree of partitioned parallelism for each operator so as to fully utilize the disk and all CPUs.

Many other efforts in parallel query optimization [SE93, LST91, SYT93, CLYY92, HLY93, ZZBS93] develop heuristics assuming parallel execution to have no extra cost.

2. Price of Parallelism

This chapter is a case study of NonStop SQL/MP, a commercial parallel DBMS from Tandem Computers[1]. We report experimental measurements of the overheads in parallel execution as compared to sequential execution[2]. We also document the use of parallel execution techniques in a commercial system.

Our experiments investigate two overheads of using parallel execution: startup and communication. Startup is the overhead of obtaining and initializing the set of processes used to execute the query. Communication is the overhead of communicating data among these processes while executing the query. The findings from the experiments may be summarized as:

• Startup costs are negligible if processes can be *reused* rather than created afresh.

• Communication cost consists of the CPU cost of sending and receiving messages.

• Communication costs can exceed the cost of operators such as scanning, joining or grouping

These findings lead to the important conclusion that

> *Query optimization should be concerned with communication costs but not with startup costs.*

2.1 Introduction

Startup overhead is incurred as a prelude to real work. It consists of obtaining a set of processes and passing to each a description of its role in executing the query. The description consists of the portion of the query plan the process

---

[1] We thank Tandem Computers for providing access to NonStop SQL/MP and a parallel machine. Parts of this chapter have also been published as the paper *S. Englert, R. Glasstone and W. Hasan: Parallelism and its Price: A Case Study of NonStop SQL/MP, Sigmod Record, Dec 1995*

[2] We used the following guidelines to prevent commercial misuse of our experimental results: (a) All execution times are scaled by a fixed but unspecified factor. (b) All query executions were created by bypassing the NonStop SQL optimizer and no inference should be drawn about its behavior.

will execute and the identities of the other processes it will communicate with.

Communication overhead is the cost of transferring data between processes. Our experiments consider three categories of communication between processes. *Local* communication consists of a producer process sending data to a consumer process on the same processor. *Remote* communication is the case when the producer and consumer are on distinct processors. *Repartitioned* communication consists of a set of producers sending data to a set of consumers. Each tuple is routed based on the value of some attribute.

Communication requires data to be moved from one physical location to another. Local communication is implemented as a memory to memory copy across address spaces. Remote communication divides data into packets that are transmitted across the interconnect. The receiving CPU has to process interrupts generated by packet arrival as well as to reassemble the data. In repartitioned communication, a producer has to perform some additional computation to determine the destination of each tuple.

Our experiments compare the cost of communication with the cost of operators such as scans, joins and groupings. We observe that while the cost of communicating data is proportional to the number of bytes transmitted, an operator may not even look at all its input data – it only needs to look at attributes that are relevant to it and may ignore the attributes that are relevant only to subsequent operators.

We first describe the architecture of Tandem systems in Section 2.2. In Section 2.3, we describe how opportunities for parallelism are exploited by NonStop SQL/MP. We then describe our experimental results on startup costs in Section 2.4. Section 2.5 describes our results on the cost of communication. These costs are put in perspective by comparing them with costs of operators such as scans, joins and groupings. Section 2.6 shows interesting examples of parallel and sequential execution and Section 2.7 summarizes our conclusions.

2.2 Tandem Architecture: An Overview

2.2.1 Parallel and Fault-Tolerant Hardware

Tandem systems are fault-tolerant, parallel machines. For the purpose of query processing, a Tandem system may be viewed as a classical shared-nothing system (see Figure 2.1). Each processor has local memory and exclusive control over some subset of the disks.

Processors communicate over an interconnection network. Up to 16 processors may be connected to an interprocessor bus to form a *node*. A variety of technologies and topologies are used to interconnect multiple nodes.

For fault-tolerance, each logical disk consists of a mirrored pair of physical disks. Disk controllers ensure that a write request is executed on both disks.

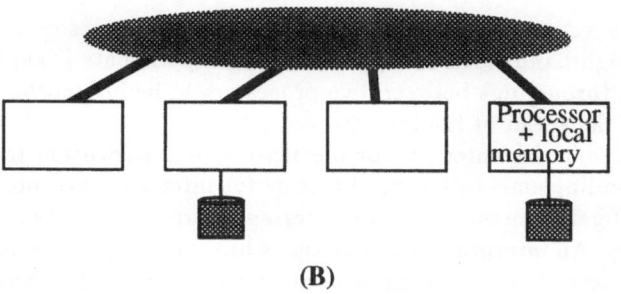

Fig. 2.1. (A) Tandem Architecture (B) Abstraction as Shared-Nothing

A read request is directed to the disk that can service it faster; for example if both disks are idle, the request is directed to the one with its read head closer to the data.

We will not discuss further fault-tolerance features of the Tandem architecture since they are largely orthogonal to query processing. The interested reader is referred to [BBT88] for details.

2.2.2 Message Based Software

Messages implement interprocess communication as well as disk IO. Access to a disk is encapsulated by an associated set of disk processes that run on the processor that controls the disk. They implement the basic facilities for reading, writing and locking disk-resident data. An IO request is made by sending a message to a disk process. Data read by a read request is also sent back to the requester as a message. Use of a set of disk processes allows several requests to be processed concurrently. Disk processes are system processes and, for the purpose of query processing, may be regarded as being permanently in operation.

A single file may be partitioned across multiple disks by ranges of key values. This allows tables and indexes to be horizontally partitioned using range partitioning. The file system is cognizant of partitioned files and can route messages based on the key value of a requested record.

2.2.3 Performance Characteristics

The interconnect used for communication between processors is engineered to provide high bandwidth and performance. Experiments [Tan] have shown the message throughput between two processors to be limited by CPU speed rather than the speed of the interprocessor bus.

The programming interface for messages provides location transparency. However, the implementation mechanisms for inter and intraprocessor messages are different. An intraprocessor message is transmitted by a memory-to-memory copy. An interprocessor message is broken into packets and sent over the interconnect. Packet arrival generates interrupts at the receiving CPU. The packets are then assembled and written into the memory of the receiving process. Measurements show an intraprocessor message to be significantly cheaper than an interprocessor message.

A mirrored disk consists of two physical disks with identical data layout. As remarked earlier, a write request is executed on both physical disks while a read is directed to the disk that can process it faster. A mirrored pair processes read requests faster than a single physical disk while write requests run at about the same speed.

2.3 Parallelism in NonStop SQL/MP

NonStop SQL/MP uses intra-operator parallelism for scans, selection, projection, joins and grouping and aggregation. Intra-operation parallelism uses replication as well as partitioning. Inter-operator parallelism is not used. The system does not, for example, use pipelined parallelism, in which *disjoint* sets of processors are used for the producer and consumer. It does, however, use pipelined execution whenever possible, in which producers and consumers run concurrently (on the same processor)

In Section 2.3.1, we discuss the use of intra-operator parallelism. Section 2.3.2 discusses how operators are mapped to a processes and processes to processors.

2.3.1 Use of Intra-operator Parallelism

Intra-operator parallelism is based on data partitioning and replication. Recall that base tables and indexes may be stored horizontally partitioned over several disks based on key ranges. Scans and groupings are parallelized using the existing data partitioning.

Joins may repartition or replicate data in addition to using the existing data partitioning. Such repartitioning or replication occurs on the fly while processing a query and does not affect any stored data. Data repartitioning is based on hashing and equally distributes data across *all* CPUs.

Stored data is scanned by disk processes that implement selection, projection and some kinds of groupings and aggregation. Since each disk has its exclusive disk processes, the architecture naturally supports parallel scans.

Grouping is implemented in two ways, one based on sorting and the other on hashing. Sort grouping first sorts the data on the grouping columns and then computes the grouped aggregates by traversing the tuples in order. Hash grouping forms groups by building a hash table based on the grouping columns and then computes aggregates for each group.

The strategy for parallelizing a grouping is to use the existing data partitioning. A separate grouping is done for each partition followed by a combination of the results. Data is *not* repartitioned to change the degree of parallelism or the partitioning attribute.

A join of two tables (say T and S) may be parallelized in the following two ways corresponding to Equations 1.2 and 1.1.

Partition Both: Both tables may be partitioned only when an equijoin predicate is available. If both tables are similarly partitioned on the join column, the "matching" partitions may be joined. Otherwise, one or both tables may be repartitioned.

Partition and Replicate: Another parallelization strategy is to partition S and join each partition of S with all of table T. This may be achieved in two ways. The first is to replicate T on all nodes that contain a partition of S. The second is to *repartition* S (for example, to increase degree of parallelism) and replicate T on all nodes with a (new) partition of S.

Three methods are used for joins: nested-loops, sort-merge and hybrid-hash. Table 2.1 summarizes the join methods used for each parallelization strategy.

When both tables happen to be partitioned similarly by the join column, sort-merge join is the most efficient join method. Since the partitioning columns are always identical to the sequencing columns in NonStop SQL, the sorting step of sort-merge is skipped and the matching partitions are simply merged.

In the strategy of repartitioning both tables, both are distributed across all CPUs using a hash function on the joining columns. In this way, corresponding data from both tables or composites is located such that it can be joined locally in each CPU using the hybrid-hash join method. The strategy of repartitioning only one of the tables is not considered.

The partition-and-replicate strategy considers nested-loops as well as hybrid-hash. The inner table is replicated and the outer table is partitioned. If the existing partitioning of the outer is used, then both nested-loops and hybrid-hash are considered. If the outer is repartitioned, then only hybrid-hash is considered.

Nested-loops join is implemented by sending a message to lookup the inner table for each tuple of the outer (thus incurring random IO in accessing the inner). The inner is replicated in the sense that if two tuples in different partitions of the outer have the same value of the join attribute, then the matching tuples of the inner will get sent to both partitions. Thus, only the relevant portion of the inner table is accessed and replication of tuples happens only if needed.

When used with partition-and-replicate parallelization, hybrid-hash join replicates the inner table. Either the existing partitioning of the outer is used or the outer is repartitioned across all CPUs. A hash table is built on the inner at each participating CPU and subsequently probed by tuples from the inner. When used with partition-both parallelization, both tables are repartitioned across all CPUs. The hybrid-hash join algorithm has adaptive aspects such as adjusting to the amount of available memory. The interested reader is referred to Zeller and Gray [ZG90] for details.

Nested-loops accesses only the relevant tuples of the inner table. Since hybrid-hash accesses the entire inner, it avoids the random IO incurred by nested-loops but also accesses tuples of the inner that may not join. Nested-loops is the only applicable method when there is no equijoin predicate.

2.3.2 Process Structure

A single SQL query is executed by use of multiple processes. Three kinds of processes are used. First, there is the SQL *Executor* process, which consists

	Partition Both		Partition and Replicate	
	Use Existing Partitioning	Repartition both	Existing Partitioning for one replicate other	Repartition one replicate other
hybrid-hash	×	√	√	√
nested-loops	×	×	√	×
Sort-merge	√	×	×	×

KEY: √ indicates use of strategy for join method, × indicates not used.

Table 2.1. Parallelization Strategies and Join Methods

of system library routines bound into the user application. Second, slave processes called ESPs (for Executor Server Process) may be spawned by the Executor. Third, there are disk processes which are system processes that are permanently in operation.

Scans are implemented by disk processes and the remaining work is divided between ESPs and the Executor. The query result is produced by the Executor. The mapping of operators to processes and allocation of processes to processors may be understood with respect to query trees in which interior nodes represent operations such as joins and groupings and leaves represent scans. The basic idea in forming processes is to have an operator share processes with the prior (child) operator as far as possible. New processes are created only when such combination is impossible due to a data repartitioning or due to the fact that the prior operator is a scan. In the case of a join there are two children. Since once of them is always a base table or index, the join is attempted to be combined with the operator that produces the outer table.

Scans (the leaves of a query tree) are always executed by disk processes. Thus scans are parallelized based on the partitioning of the data being read; there is one process for each disk that contains a partition of the data. While ESPs are capable of repartitioning their output, disk processes are not. Thus if the result of a scan is to be repartitioned, one ESP is created per existing partition of the data for the sole purpose of repartitioning data.

A grouping is always parallelized based on the existing partitioning of the data. It can be combined into the same process as the prior operator, unless the prior operator is a scan and the grouping is such that a disk process cannot implement it. Disk processes can implement groupings in which the grouping columns are a prefix of the key columns.

The process structure for joins is more complex since a join has two operands. One of the operands, the inner, is always a base table. For nested-loops and merge-join, one ESP is used per partition of the outer table. If possible, this ESP is the same ESP as for the operator that produces the outer table. The inner is accessed by sending messages to disk processes. In the case of nested-loops, one message is sent per tuple of the outer so as to retrieve only the relevant tuples.

We only describe the process structure of hybrid-hash for the case when both operands are repartitioned. One ESP is used per existing partition of the inner to repartition data. If the outer is a base table, one new ESP is used per partition of the outer to repartition data. On the other hand, if the outer is not a base table, then the ESP that produces it also performs the repartitioning. One ESP is used at each CPU to receive the repartitioned data and locally compute a hybrid-hash join.

2.4 Startup Costs

Parallel execution requires starting up a set of processes and communicating data among them. This section measures startup cost and the next section focuses on communication.

When a query is executed in parallel, the Executor process starts up all necessary ESP processes and sends to each the portion of the plan it needs to execute and the identities of the other processes it needs to communicate with. The ESP processes are created sequentially; each process is created and given its plan before the next process is created. ESPs are not terminated for 5 minutes after the query completes. In case another query is executed within five minutes, ESP processes are reused.

We measured the cost of starting up processes by running a query that required 44 ESP processes. Figure 2.2 plots the time at which successive processes got started and had received their portion of the plan. The dotted line plots process startup when new processes had to be created. The solid line plots the case when processes were reused.

We conclude that communicating the relevant portion of the plan to each ESP has negligible cost. Startup cost is negligible when processes can be reused. Startup incurs an overhead of 0.5 sec per process that needs to be created. A possible enhancement would be to start the ESP processes in parallel instead of sequentially.

2.5 Costs of Operators and Communication

In this section we measure the cost of communication and put these costs in perspective by a comparison with operators such as scans, joins and grouping.

We describe measurements of the cost of local, remote and repartitioned communication. Local communication consists of a producer process sending data to a consumer process on the same processor. Remote communication is the case when the producer and consumer are on distinct processors. In repartitioned communication, a set of producers send data to a set of producers. The cost of repartitioning varies with the pattern of communication used. We decided to focus on the case where a *single* producer partitions its output

Elapsed Time (seconds)

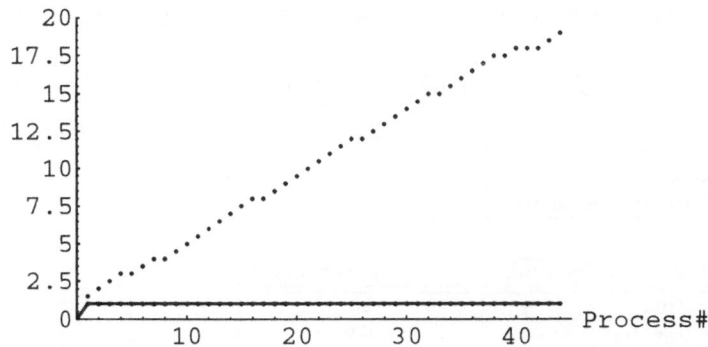

Fig. 2.2. Process Startup: With (Solid) and Without (Dotted) Process Reuse.

equally among a set of consumers. This simple pattern captures the overhead of a producer sending data to multiple consumers i.e. the additional overhead of determining the the destination of each tuple. The producer applies a hash function to an attribute value to determine the CPU to which the tuple is to be sent. Figure 2.3 illustrates the forms of communication covered by our experiments. These cases were chosen due to their simplicity. The costs of other communication patterns may be extrapolated.

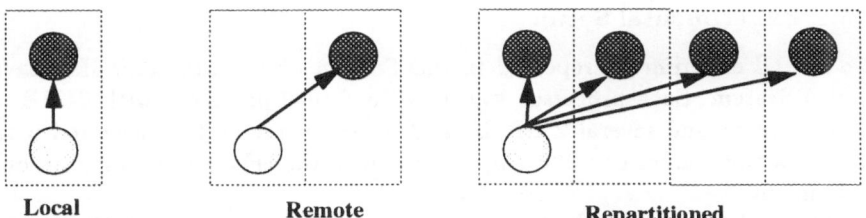

Local   Remote   Repartitioned

Fig. 2.3. Local, Remote and Repartitioned Communication

Table 2.2 summarizes the results of measurements that are described later in this section. It turned out that the cpu time of all our queries was linear in the amount of data accessed. Even operations that involved sorting behaved linearly in the range covered by our experiments. Thus costs are stated in units of msec/Ktuple and msec/Mbyte. The two units are comparable, since 1K tuples occupy 1 Mbyte for the table under consideration. Join costs were measured by joining two tables, each with k tuples, to produce k output tuples. Join costs were linear in k and are therefore reported in msec/Ktuple.

Transfer Operation	Cost (msec/Mbyte)
Scan	180
Local Comm.	390
Remote Comm.	745
Repartitioning (4 CPUs)	1230

Computational Operation	Cost (msec/Ktuple)
Aggregation	65
Sort-Merge Join	370
Hash Join	40
Hash Grouping	110
Sort Grouping	765

Table 2.2. CPU Costs of Transfer and Computational Operations. (1K Tuples Occupy 1 Mbyte)

Our approach was to devise experiments such that the cost of an operation could be determined as the difference of two executions. For instance the cost of local communication was determined as the difference of executing the same query using two plans that only differed in whether one or two processes were used.

Section 2.5.1 gives an overview of our experimental setup. Sections 2.5.3 and 2.5.4 describe experiments that measure the cost of communication and Sections 2.5.2, 2.5.5 and 2.5.6 address the costs of operators.

2.5.1 Experimental Setup

We ran all experiments reported in this Section on a 4 processor Himalaya K1000 System. Each processor was a MIPS R3000 processor with 64MB of main memory and several 2 GB disks. The size of the cache associated with each disk was reduced to 300 Kbytes to reduce the effects of caching on our experiments.

The tables Single, Single2 and Quad used in our experiments had identical schema and content. Quad was equally partitioned over four disks while Single and Single2 were stored on single disks.

Each of these tables had four columns: unique, twenty, hundred and str. The first three were integer columns and the fourth a 988 byte string. The unique column was the key and each table was stored sorted by this column. The column twenty was randomly chosen from 1...20, hundred randomly chosen from 1...100, and str was a 988 byte string with an identical value in each row. Each tuple occupied 1000 bytes. Each table had 50,000 tuples resulting in a total size of 50 Mbytes.

We forced query plans by the use of optimizer hooks that allowed us to specify plan elements such as the sequence and method for each join; whether parallel execution should be used or not; and whether a join should repartition data or not, whether predicates should be combined with a disk process or not and so on. The EXPLAIN command in NonStop SQL allowed us to view plans to confirm the details of the execution.

We collected performance data by using MEASURE, a low overhead tool. MEASURE collects statistics about objects of interest such as processors, disks, processes and files while a program is in execution. The collected statistics can later be perused using a query tool. MEASURE also measures the cost of processing interrupts that are generated by message arrival and IO completions – these costs are not assigned to any process.

Each data point reported in this paper is an average over three executions. Typically, the three executions differed by less than 1%. All plotted curves were obtained using a least squares fit using the Fit function in Mathematica.

2.5.2 Costs of Scans, Predicates and Aggregation

We used the following query to scan Single.

Query1:   select unique from Single
             where twenty > 50000 and unique < k

The predicate twenty >50000 is false for all tuples. Thus no tuples are returned and the overhead of communicating the result of the scan is eliminated. Since the table was stored sorted by unique, the predicate unique < k allowed us to vary the portion of the table scanned.

The query plan used a single disk process and combined predicate evaluation with the scan. The cost of the plan consists of a scan and two predicate evaluations, one of which is a key predicate. The dotted line in Figure 2.4 plots the cost as k was varied from 5000 to 50000 in increments of 5000. Denoting cpu cost by t and the number of Mbytes scanned by b, a least squares fit yields the equation $t = 0.31 + 0.185b$. Thus a scan with two predicates costs 185 msec/Mbyte.

We determined the cost of predicate checking by additional measurements. To measure the cost of the key predicate, we tried two queries: one with the predicate unique < 100,000 and the other with no key predicate. Both queries scanned the entire table, since all key values were less than 100,000, and ran in identical time.

To measure the cost of the nonkey predicate, we ran a query with *two* nonkey predicates. The "where clause" of Query1 was changed to (twenty >50000 or hundred >50000) and unique1 < k. The solid lines in Figure 2.4 plots the cost of a query. Curve fitting yields $t = 0.31 + 0.18b$ i.e. the cost increases by 5 msec/Mbyte due to the additional nonkey predicate. Thus, we may expect a scan with *no* predicates to cost 180 msec/Mbyte.

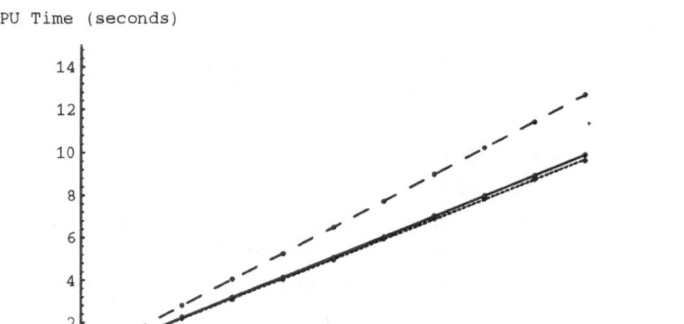

CPU Time (seconds)

Fig. 2.4. Scan with 1 Predicate (Dotted), 2 Predicates (Solid), Aggregation (Dashed)

The dashed line in Figure 2.4 shows the cost of applying an aggregation in the disk process using the following query.

Query2:   select max(str) from Single
                     where unique < k

A least square fit yielded the equation $t = 0.31 + 0.245b$. Subtracting scan cost, we infer aggregation to cost (245-180) msec/Mbyte which is 65 msec/Mbyte. Recall that str is a 988 byte string with an identical value in each row. Thus the aggregation uses 988 bytes of each 1000 byte tuple.

2.5.3 Costs of Local and Remote Communication

We measured the cost of local and remote communication by use of optimizer hooks that permitted the creation of plans in which the aggregation in Query2 was moved to a separate process (the Executor) and the process could either be placed on the same CPU as the disk process or on a different CPU. Figure 2.6 shows the process structure for the three executions.

When aggregation is in a separate process from scan, 988 bytes of each 1000 byte tuple have to be communicated across processes. Figure 2.5(A) plots the data points for scanning and aggregation in the disk process and also with the remote and local communication. The cases (A), (B) and (C) in the figure correspond to the three process organizations of Figure 2.6. Least squares curve fitting shows slopes of 0.635 and 0.99 for the local and remote curves. Since scanning and aggregation without communication has a slope of 0.245, we infer that local communication costs 390 msec/Mbyte and remote communication costs 745 msec/Mbyte.

We observe that the relative cost of communication is a function of the amount of data communicated. Figure 2.5(b) shows the case when Query2 is modified to aggregate on twenty. In this case only 4 bytes of each 1000

CPU Time

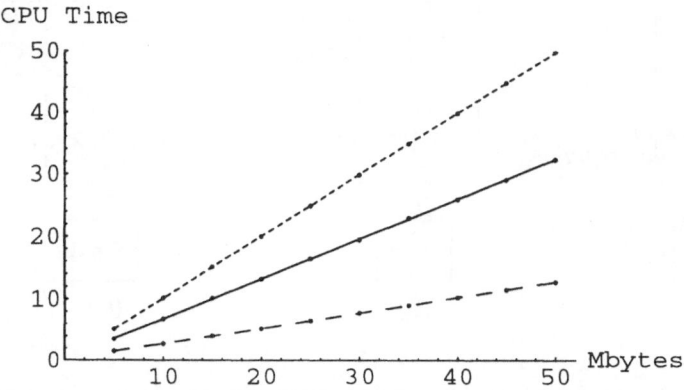

(i) **98.8%** of scanned data communicated. Curves from bottom to top are
(A) Cost of Scan+Aggregation using single process
(B) Cost of Scan+Aggregation using two processes with local communication
(C) Cost of Scan+Aggregation using two processes with remote communication.

CPU Time

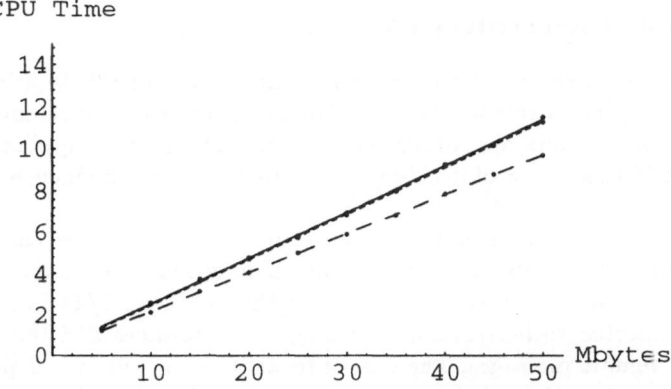

(ii) **4%** of scanned data communicated. Curves from bottom to top are
(A) Cost of Scan+Aggregation using single process
(B) Cost of Scan+Aggregation using two processes with local communication
(C) Cost of Scan+Aggregation using two processes with remote communication.

Fig. 2.5. Scan and Aggregation

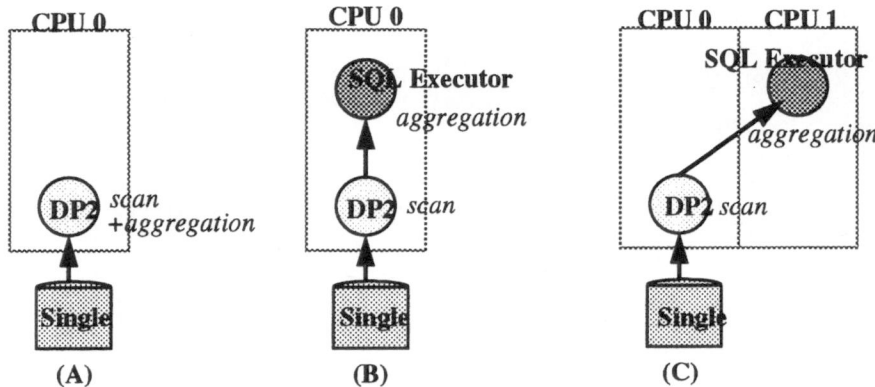

Fig. 2.6. Process Structure: (A) No Communication (B) Local (C) Remote

byte tuple have to be communicated across processes and the relative cost of communication is negligible.

2.5.4 Cost of Repartitioned Communication

Repartitioning dynamically distributes data across all CPUs using a hash function. In general this involves a combination of local and remote communication. Since tuples are routed based on a hash function applied to some column, additional cost of deciding the destination must be incurred for each tuple.

Given a system with 4 CPUs, we chose to focus on the case where a single producer equally repartitions data among four consumers. Since one consumer was placed on the same CPU as the producer, 1/4'th of the tuples may be expected to be transported using local messages and the remaining 3/4'th by remote messages. The cost of repartitioning will vary depending on the number of CPUs and the arrangement of producers and consumers.

We devised the following query to create two executions that only differ in whether or not data is repartitioned. Small is a single column table with twenty values 0..19 stored in twenty tuples. The result of joining Single and Small is identical to Single and is grouped into twenty groups.

Query3:   select **max**(str) **from** Single w, Small s
            where w.twenty = s.unique and w.unique < k
            group by w.twenty

We forced the two executions shown in Figure 2.7. Both use a simple hash join in which a hash table is built on Small and probed by Single. The hash join is followed by a hash grouping. The first execution executes the join and grouping in the Executor process on a single CPU. The second execution build a hash table on Small and replicates it on four CPUs. Then Single is repartitioned and the join and grouping computed separately for each partition. Finally, the Executor process merges the results of the separate groupings.

While Figure 2.7(b) shows several extra communication arrows, only the repartitioning arrows are significant. Between 5 and 50 Mbytes of data is repartitioned. In comparison, the hash table on Small occupies about 0.00008 Mbytes, so replicating it has negligible cost. The result of each grouping consists of 20 groups that occupy about 0.02 Mbytes, which is comparatively negligible.

Figure 2.8 plots the costs of the two executions as as k was varied from 5000 to 50000 in increments of 5000. Least squares curve fitting shows the slopes of the lines to be 0.785 and 2.015. Since the difference between the two executions is the cost of repartitioning, we conclude repartitioning to cost $(2.015 - 0.785)$ sec/Mbyte or 1230 msec/Mbyte. We remind the reader that our measurements of repartitioning cost are for four CPUs.

2.5.5 Costs of Join Operators

We measured the cost of simple-hash, sort-merge and nested joins by joining Single with an identical copy called Single2. We executed the following query using different join methods. The query was modified for sort-merge join to require sorting on one operand by changing the join predicate to w1.unique = w2.hundred. Figure 2.9 plots the execution costs as k was varied from 5000 to 50000 in increments of 5000.

Query4: Select max(w1.str) from Single w1, Single2 w2
where w1.unique = w2.unique and
w1.unique < k and w2.unique < k

Surprisingly *all* plots in Figure 2.9 are linear in k even though we are joining two operands each with k tuples, and producing a result consisting of k tuples.

The nested join accesses the inner table (Single2) for each tuple of the outer (Single). Thus the cost is linear in the size of the outer table. Each access to the inner table is a random IO which explains the high cost of the nested join.

Hash-join builds a hash table on the qualifying tuples of Single2 and probes it using tuples from Single. The one possible source of nonlinearity is when k probes are performed on a hash table that contains k entries. We conclude that cost of a probe is independent of hash table size.

For sort-merge join, only one operand (Single2) needed to be sorted since the other was pre-sorted on the join column. It may be surprising that the cost of sorting does not introduce any nonlinear component into the cost. The explanation is that the system chose to sort by inserting tuples into a

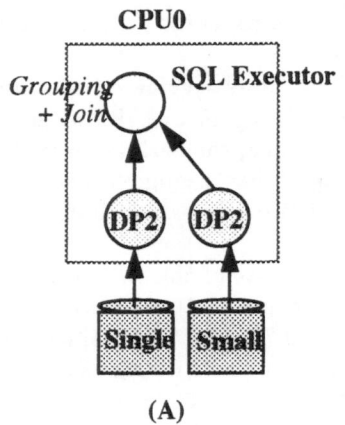

(A)

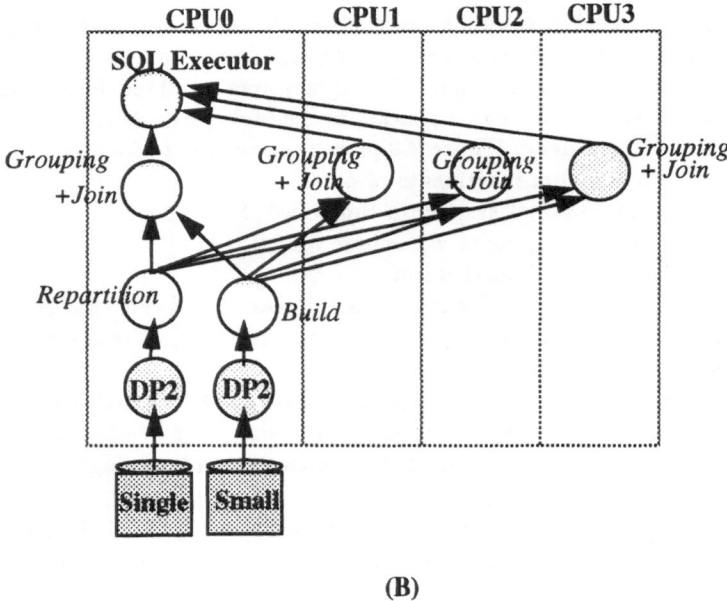

(B)

Fig. 2.7. Local and Repartitioned Execution

CPU Time (seconds)

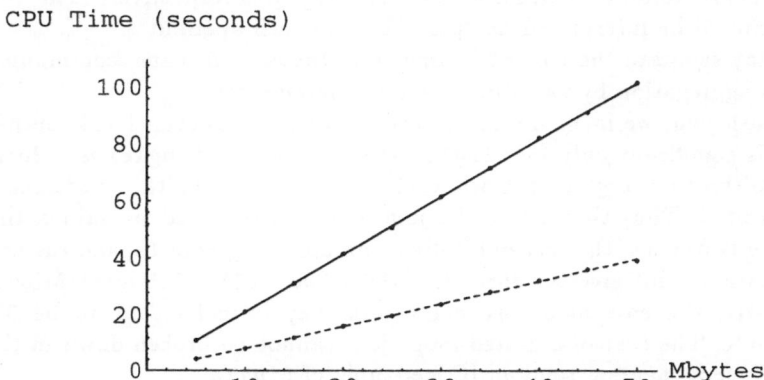

Fig. 2.8. Local (Dotted) and Repartitioned (Solid) Communication

CPU Time (seconds)

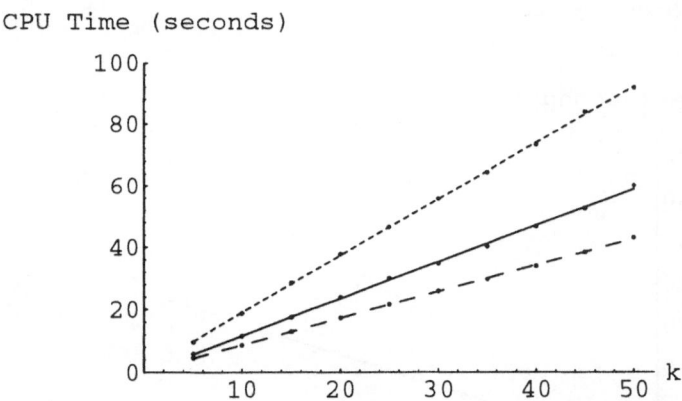

Fig. 2.9. Query Using Simple-Hash (Dashed), Sort-Merge (Solid) and Nested Join (Dotted)

sequenced file. The cost of insertion is independent of file size and the cost of comparisons is not a significant cost in locating the correct page.

Least squares curve fitting shows cost of the query to be 1835, 855 and 1185 msec/Mbyte for nested, hash and sort-merge join respectively. The "per Mbyte" should be interpreted as "per Mbyte of each operand".

We may separate the cost of joining from the cost of scans, communication, and aggregation by using our prior measurements.

For hash-join, we incur a scan for each operand. However, local communication is significant only for Single. After projection, Single2 is reduced to 4/1000'th of its original size while almost all (992/1000'th) of Single is communicated. Thus the cost of the join may be calculated by subtracting the cost of two scans, the cost of locally communicating Single, and the cost of aggregation. This gives us $855 - (2 * 180 + 390 + 65) = 105$ msec/Mbyte.

Similarly, the cost of a sort-merge join may be calculated to be 370 msec/Mbyte. The cost of a nested-loops join cannot be broken down in this manner since it incurs a random IO per tuple of Single.

2.5.6 Costs of Grouping Operators

NonStop SQL uses two algorithms for grouping. Hash grouping forms groups by hashing tuples into a hash table based on the value of the grouping column. Sort grouping forms groups by sorting the table on the grouping column. The following query reads k records and forms twenty groups.

Query5:   select **max**(str) **from** Single
          where unique $< k$
          group by twenty;

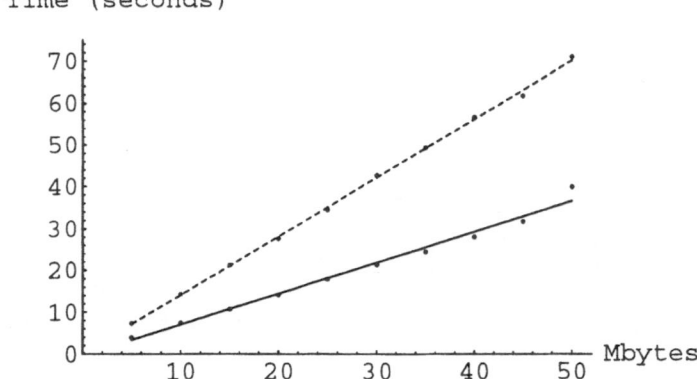

Fig. 2.10. Hash (Solid) and Sort (Dotted) Grouping Costs

Figure 2.10 plots the costs of hash and sort grouping as a function of k. Least squares curve fitting shows the query to cost 1245 msec/Mbyte and 1400 msec/Mbyte respectively for hash and sort grouping. Since the query incurs a scan, local communication, and aggregation, we conclude that hash and sort grouping to cost 110 msec/Mbyte and 765 msec/Mbyte respectively.

2.6 Parallel Versus Sequential Execution

The distinction between parallel and sequential execution in Tandem systems is the use of multiple versus single *SQL Executor* processes to execute a query. Note that sequential execution may use multiple disk processes if it accesses data from multiple disks.

Parallel and sequential execution may be compared based on two metrics: work and response time. The common intuition is that parallel execution reduces response time at the expense of increased work. The basis for this intuition is that parallel execution will cost at least much as sequential execution and will run at least as fast as sequential execution. While true in some cases, this is *not true* in general. The relative costs of parallel and sequential execution depend on communication costs.

We present two examples in this section. The first shows that parallel execution can *reduce* both work and response time by saving communication costs. The second shows that parallel execution can result in *increased* response time when the communication costs offset the benefit from parallel execution. We are not aware of any instances of the remaining logical possibility of parallel execution offering reduced work but increased response time compared to sequential execution.

To sum up, in addition to the intuitive case in which parallel execution runs faster but consumes more resources, it is possible that (a) parallel execution consumes less resources as well as runs faster and (b) parallel execution consumes more resources as well as runs slower. The main determinant is the cost of communication.

2.6.1 Parallelism Can Reduce Work

The following query performs a grouping on a table that is equally partitioned across 4 disks, each attached to a distinct CPU.

Query6:   select max(str)
           from Quad
           group by twenty;

Figure 2.11 shows the process structure for sequential and parallel execution. When sequential execution is used, SQL runs as a single process (Executor). This process must incur remote communication to read the three

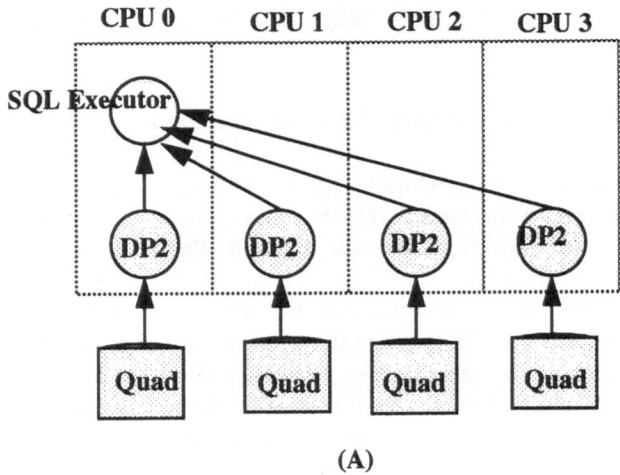

(A)

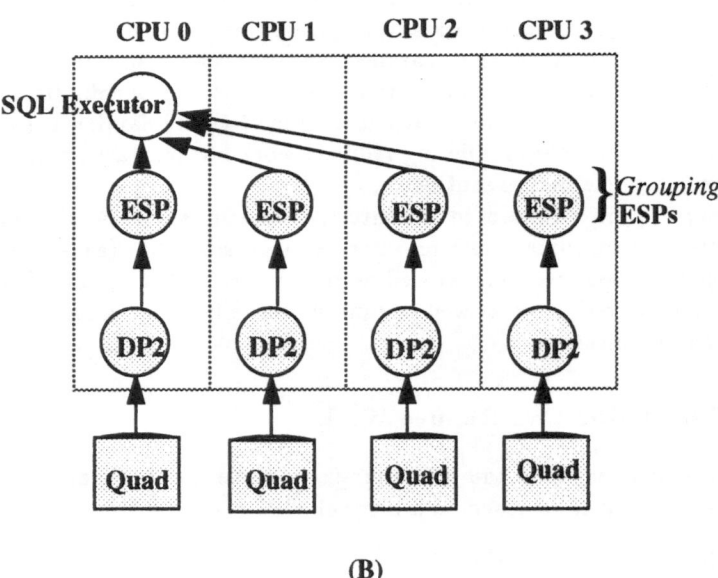

(B)

Fig. 2.11. Process Structure: Sequential and Parallel Execution

partitions that reside on remote disks. When parallel execution is used, the grouping is partitioned. Each partition of Quad is grouped separately by an ESP process. The result of each grouping is communicated to the Executor to produce the combined grouping. The local grouping at each CPU substantially reduces the amount of data to be communicated resulting in reduced work. Response time is reduced both because of work reduction as well as better load balancing.

When sequential execution was used the query used 49 sec CPU and had a response time of 78 sec. With parallel execution, the total CPU time fell to 36.5 sec and the response time fell to 26.5 sec.

2.6.2 Parallelism Can Increase Response Time

Consider the query used in Section 2.5.4 with the sequential and parallel executions shown in Figure 2.7. The parallel execution incurs greater work due to communication costs. Its response time is also increased since the parallelism available in the plan does not suffice to offset the increased work.

Consider the data point for $k = 50000$. When sequential execution was used the query used 39 sec CPU and had a response time of 66.5 sec. With parallel execution, the total CPU time rose to 102 sec and the response time rose to 109.5 sec.

Surprisingly, the response time increases to 109.5 sec even though 102/4 is less than 39. The explanation lies in the fact that there are sequential portions of the query, and the benefit from parallelism is offset by communication costs for the parallel portions. Scanning and repartitioning Single is inherently sequential. These operations can only be performed on CPU 0. Parallel execution only benefits the join and grouping. That speedup is not sufficient to offset the increase in work due to repartitioning. No parallelism is available in scanning Small and building and replicating a hash table on it. However, these operations had negligible cost compared to the rest of the query.

It should be noted that the inherent sequentiality illustrated in this example is not pathological. Selection predicates can localize a scan to a single disk (or a subset of the disks) even when a table is partitioned across several disks.

2.7 Summary of Findings

The important conclusion from our experiments is that a query optimizer should be concerned with communication costs but not with startup costs.

This is based on the following findings:

– Startup costs are negligible when processes can be *reused* rather than created afresh.

- Communication cost consists of the CPU cost of sending and receiving messages.
- Communication costs can exceed the cost of operations such as scans, joins or grouping.

Our experiments show that the cost of parallel execution can differ substantially from that of sequential execution. The cost may be more or even less depending on what data needs to be communicated.

It is worth observing that the cost of communication relative to the cost of operators is a strong function of the quality of the implementation. For example if operators are poorly implemented, communication costs will be relatively low. Further, such a poor implementation may actually lead to the system exhibiting good scalability! This underlines the fact that scalability must be tested with respect to the *best* implementation on a *uniprocessor*.

An interesting question is how communication can be avoided or its cost reduced. Architectural techniques such as DMA are likely to help to some extent. However, most of the cost of communications tends to be incurred at software levels that are higher than DMA interfaces. Use of shared-memory is of limited value since the cost of communication through a shared piece of memory rises as the number of processors increases.

3. JOQR Optimizations

In this chapter[1] we develop models and algorithms for the JOQR phase that minimize the total cost of computing a query. The models take a "macro" view of query execution. They focus on exploiting physical properties such as the partitioning of data across nodes; determination of the best combination of methods for computing operators; and fixing the order of joins. "Micro" decisions about allocation of resources are the responsibility of the subsequent parallelization phase.

We start with a simple model that captures the communication incurred when data needs to be repartitioned across processors. Minimizing communication is posed as a tree coloring problem (related to classical Multiway Cut problems [DJP+92]) in which colors represent data partitioning.

We then enhance the model in two ways. Firstly, we generalize colors to represent any collection of physical properties (such as sort-order, indexes) that can be exploited in computing an operator. Secondly, we permit each operator to have several alternate methods by which it can be computed. This allows us to captures effects such as the fact that a Grouping may be computed very efficiently if the data is partitioned as well as sorted on the grouping attribute.

The final enhancement of the model is to allow joins to be reordered. At the end of the chapter, we describe several ways in which the algorithms may be used.

It is appropriate to contrast the models and algorithms in this chapter with work in conventional query optimization [SAC+79]. Besides incorporating communication costs, our contribution is to show that choosing methods and physical properties can be *separated* from join ordering. While join ordering requires exponential time, methods and physical properties can be chosen in polynomial time. Further, join ordering only applies to joins. The algorithms for choosing physical properties and methods are applicable to any query tree. This opens up new ways of combining the different aspects of query optimization even for conventional systems.

---

[1] Parts of this chapter have been published in the two papers
W. Hasan and R. Motwani: Coloring Away Communication in Parallel Query Optimization, VLDB95
S. Ganguly, W. Hasan and R. Krishnamurthy: Query Optimization for Parallel Execution, Sigmod92

3.1 A Model for Minimizing Communication

Partitioned parallelism which exploits horizontal partitioning of relations may require data to be *repartitioned* among sites thus incurring substantial communication costs.

Example 3.1.1. Assume tables Emp(enum,<u>name</u>, areaCode, number) and Cust(name,<u>areaCode</u>, number) are horizontally partitioned on two sites on the underlined attributes. The following query (in SQL2 [X3H92] syntax) determines the number of employees who are also customers in each area code. An employee and a customer are guessed to be the same person if they have the same name and phone number:
Select areaCode, Count(*)
From Cust Intersect (Select name, areaCode, number From Emp)
Group by areaCode;
Figure 3.1 shows two query trees that differ only in how data is repartitioned. Since tuples with the same areaCode need to come together, GroupBy is partitioned by areaCode. However, Intersect may be partitioned on *any* attribute. If we choose to partition it by areaCode, we will need to repartition the (projected) Emp table. If we partition by name, we will need to repartition the Cust table as well as the output of Intersect. Thus one or the other query tree may be better depending on the relative sizes of the intermediate tables.

3.1.1 Partitioning

We begin with a formal definition of partitioning.

Definition 3.1.1. *A partitioning is a pair (a, h) where a is an attribute and h is a function that maps values of a to non-negative integers.* Given a table T, a partitioning produces fragments $T_0, \ldots, T_k$

For example, the partitioning of Emp in Example 3.1.1 is represented as (name, hash(name) mod 2). The function hash(name) mod 2 is applied to each tuple of Emp and the tuple placed in fragment Emp_0 or Emp_1 depending on whether the function returns 0 or 1.

Partitioning provides a source of parallelism since the semantics of most database operators allows them to be applied in parallel to each fragment. Suppose $S_0, \ldots, S_k$ and $T_0, \ldots, T_k$ are fragments of tables S and T produced by the *same* partitioning $\alpha = (a, h)$.

Definition 3.1.2. *A unary operator f is partitionable with respect to α if and only if $f(S) = f(S_0) \cup \ldots \cup f(S_k)$. A binary operator f is partitionable with respect to α if and only if $f(S, T) = f(S_0, T_0) \cup \ldots \cup f(S_k, T_k)$.*

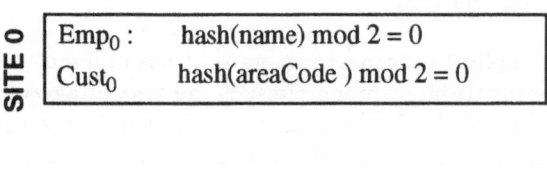

SITE 0

| Emp_0 : | hash(name) mod 2 = 0 |
| $Cust_0$ | hash(areaCode) mod 2 = 0 |

SITE 1

| Emp_1 : | hash(name) mod 2 = 1 |
| $Cust_1$ | hash(areaCode) mod 2 = 1 |

(A) Schema

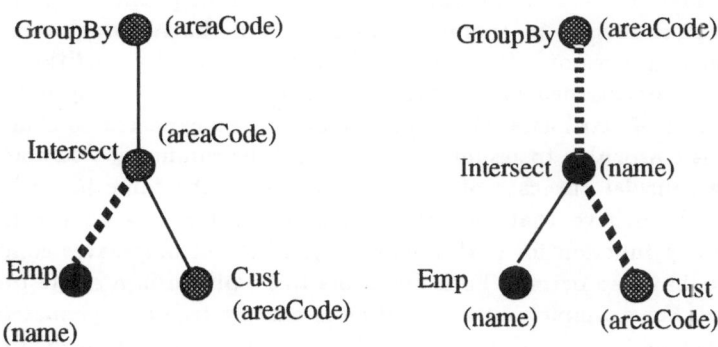

GroupBy (areaCode)

Intersect (areaCode)

Emp (name)   Cust (areaCode)

GroupBy (areaCode)

Intersect (name)

Emp (name)   Cust (areaCode)

(B) Alternate Query Trees

Fig. 3.1. Query Trees: Hatched Edges Show Repartitioning

Definition 3.1.3. *An* attribute sensitive *operator is partitionable only for partitionings that use a distinguished attribute. An* attribute insensitive *operator is partitionable for all partitionings.*

The equation $S \bowtie T = \cup_i (S_i \bowtie T_i)$ holds only if both S and T are partitioned on the (equi-)join attribute. Thus join is attribute sensitive. Similarly, *grouping* is attribute sensitive since it requires partitioning by the grouping attribute. UNION,   INTERSECT and EXCEPT (set difference), *aggregation, selection* and *projection* are attribute insensitive. External functions and predicates may be either sensitive or insensitive.

3.1.2 Repartitioning Cost

Communicating tuples between operators that use different partitionings requires redistributing tuples among sites. Some percentage of tuples remain at the same site under both partitionings and therefore do not need to be communicated across sites. We believe that the crucial determinant of the extent of communication cost, given a "good" scheduler, is the *attribute* used for partitioning. We argue the following *all or nothing* assumption to be reasonable.

Good Scheduler Assumption: *If two communicating operators use the same partitioning attribute,* no *inter-site communication is incurred. If they use distinct partitioning attributes then* all *tuples need to be communicated across sites.*

Consider the case of two operators with different partitioning attributes. The greatest savings in communication occur if the two operators use the same set of processors. If a table with m tuples equally partitioned across k sites is repartitioned on a different attribute, then assuming independent distribution of attributes, $(1 - \frac{1}{k})m$ tuples may be expected to change sites. Thus it is reasonable to assume all m tuples to be communicated across sites.

Now consider the case of two operators with the same partitioning attribute. We believe that any good scheduler will choose to use the same partitioning function for both operators since it not only saves communication cost but also permits both operators to be placed in a single process at each site. For example, our assumption is exactly true for *symmetric* schedulers (such as those used in Gamma [DGS+90]) that partition each operator equally over the same set of sites.

3.1.3 Optimization Problem

We associate colors with nodes as corresponding to the partitioning attribute.

Definition 3.1.4. *The* color *of a node in a query tree is the attribute used for partitioning the node. An edge between nodes i and j is multi-colored if and only if i and j are assigned distinct colors.*

In a query tree, the nodes for attribute sensitive operators or base tables are *pre-colored* while we have the freedom to assign colors to the remaining *uncolored* nodes.

We will associate a weight c_e with each edge e to represent the cost of repartitioning. Since this cost is incurred only if the edge is multi-colored, the total repartitioning cost is the sum of the weights of all multicolored edges. Thus the optimization problem is:

Query Tree Coloring Problem: *Given a query tree $T = (V, E)$, weight c_e for edge $e \in E$, and colors for some subset of the nodes in V, color the remaining nodes so as to minimize the total weight of multicolored edges.*

Conventional cost models [SAC$^+$79] provide estimates for the sizes of intermediate results. The weight c_e may be estimated as a function of these sizes. Our work is applicable regardless of the model used for estimation of intermediate result sizes or the function for estimation of repartitioning cost. We assume some method of estimating c_e to be available.

Query tree coloring is related to the classical problem of multiway cuts with the difference that multiway cut restricts pre-colored nodes to have distinct colors. Multiway cut is NP-hard for graphs but solvable in polynomial time for trees [DJP$^+$92]. Chopra and Rao [CR91] developed an $O(n^2)$ algorithm (where n is the number of tree nodes) for multiway cut for trees using linear programming techniques. The DLC algorithm in the next section is substantially simpler and has a running time of $O(n)$. Erdos and Szekely [ES94] provide an $O(n|C|^2)$ algorithm (where $|C|$ is number of colors) for the case of repeated colors. The ColorSplit algorithm in the next section is an $O(n|C|)$ algorithm based on a better implementation of their ideas.

Example 3.1.2. Figure 3.2(i) shows the query tree for a query to count parts used in manufacture of aircraft but not of cars or boats. The three base tables are assumed to be partitioned on distinct attributes (colors) A, B, and C. Figures 3.2(ii) and 3.2(iii) show two colorings. The cost of a coloring is the sum of the cut edges which are shown hatched. The coloring in Figure 3.2(ii) is obtained by the simple heuristic of coloring an operator so as to avoid repartitioning the most expensive operand. The minimal coloring is shown in Figure 3.2(iii); here, UNION is not partitioned on the partitioning attributes of any of its operands.

3.2 Algorithms for Query Tree Coloring

Coloring nodes may equivalently be viewed as cutting/collapsing edges. An edge between nodes of distinct colors is cut while an edge between nodes of identical colors is collapsed. This view constrains colors of adjacent nodes to be identical or distinct without fixing actual colors.

We first present some simplifications of the problem in Section 3.2.1. In Section 3.2.2, we consider the restricted problem in which all pre-colored nodes have distinct colors. We show this problem to be solvable by a simple greedy algorithm that runs in linear time. Section 3.2.3 shows the greedy algorithm to fail when colors are repeated and develops a $O(n|C|)$ dynamic programming algorithm (n is the number of tree nodes and $|C|$ the number of colors). Section 3.2.4 discusses extensions to deal with optimization opportunities provided by choices in access methods (due to indexes, replication of tables) and choices in join and grouping attributes.

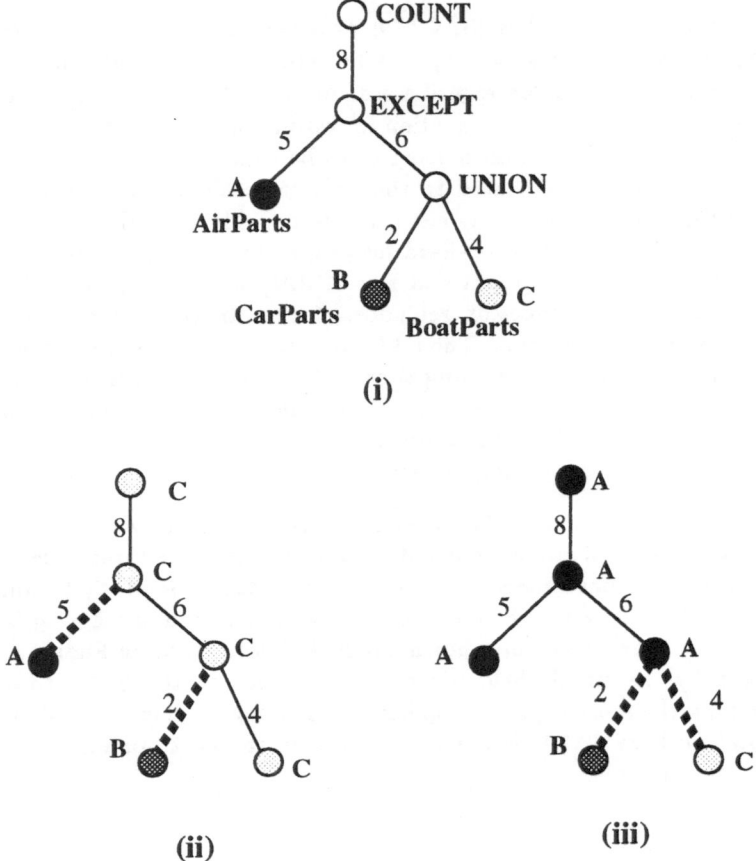

Fig. 3.2. (i) Query Tree; (ii) Coloring of Cost 7; (iii) Minimal Coloring of Cost 6

3.2.1 Problem Simplification

The problem of coloring a tree can be reduced to coloring a *set* of trees which have the special property that all interior nodes are uncolored and all leaves are pre-colored. This follows from the following observations which imply that colored interior nodes may be split into colored leaves, and uncolored leaves may be deleted.

(Split) A colored interior node of degree d may be split into d nodes of the same color and each incident edge connected to a distinct copy. This decomposes the problem into d sub-problems which can be solved independently.

(Collapse) An uncolored leaf node may be collapsed into its parent. This gives it the same color as its parent which is minimal since it incurs zero cost.

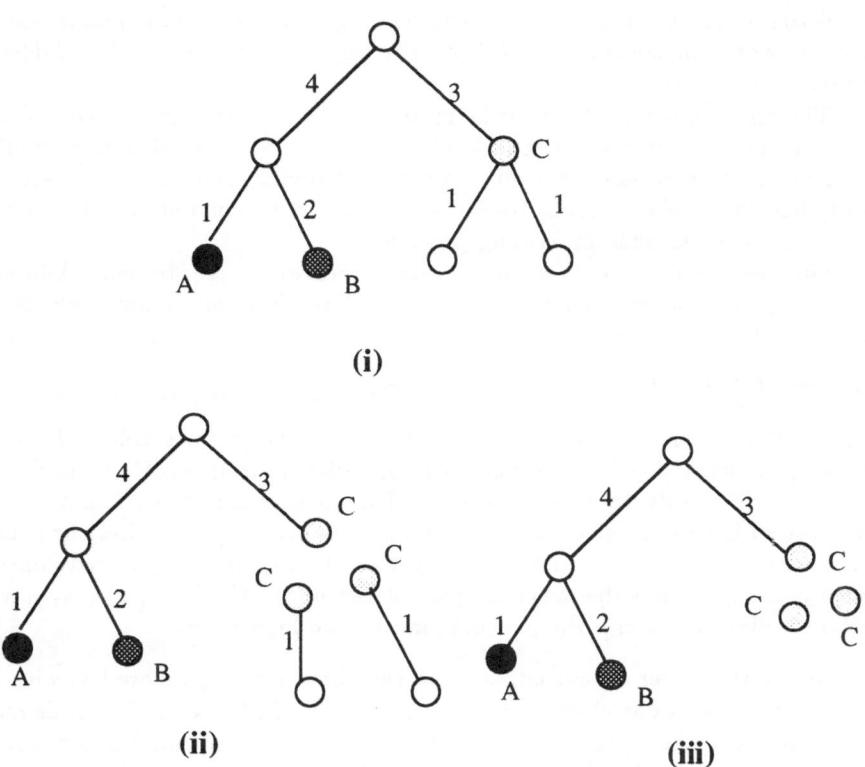

Fig. 3.3. (i) Split Colored Interior Node (ii) Collapse Uncolored Leaves

The following procedure achieves the simplified form in time linear in the number of nodes in the original tree. Figure 3.3 illustrates the simplification process.

Algorithm 1. Procedure *Simplify*

1.   **while** ∃ uncolored leaf *l* with parent *m* **do**
2.   collapse *l* with *m*;
3.   **while** ∃ colored interior node *m* with degree *d* **do**
4.   split *m* into *d* copies with each copy connected to distinct a edge.

3.2.2 A Greedy Algorithm for Distinct Pre-Colorings

We now focus on the restricted case when all pre-colored nodes have *distinct* colors. By the discussion in the previous section, we only need to consider trees in which a node is pre-colored if and only if it is a leaf node.

Definition 3.2.1. *A node is a* mother node *if and only if all adjacent nodes with at most one exception are leaves. The leaf nodes are termed the children of the mother node.*

The algorithm repeatedly picks mother nodes and processes them by either cutting or collapsing edges. Each such step creates smaller trees while preserving the invariant that all and only leaf nodes are colored. We are finally left with a set of trivial trees that may be easily colored. The following two lemmas make such processing possible.

Suppose m is a mother node with edges $e_1, \ldots, e_d$ to leaf children $v_1, \ldots, v_d$. Assume we have numbered the children in order of non-decreasing edge weight, i.e., $c_{e_1} \leq c_{e_2} \leq \cdots \leq c_{e_d}$.

Lemma 3.2.1. *There exists a minimal coloring that cuts* $e_1, \ldots, e_{d-1}$.

Proof. The proof uses the fact that all leaves have distinct colors. In any coloring at least $d - 1$ leaves have a color different from m. If the optimal colors m differently from all leaves, the lemma is clearly true. If not, then suppose m has the same color as leaf v_i and let this color be A. Let the color of v_d be B. Change all A-colored nodes (other than v_i) to be B-colored nodes. Such a change is possible since no pre-colored node other than v_i may have color A. Since $c_{e_i} \leq c_{e_d}$, the new coloring has no higher cost.

Notice that after we cut edges using the above lemma, we are left with a mother node with one child. Consider the case in which the mother node has a parent. Then the mother node is of degree 2 and the following lemma shows how we can deal with this case. Let the incident edges be e_1 and e_2 such that $c_{e_1} \leq c_{e_2}$. Since m is not pre-colored, a minimal coloring will always be able to save the cost of the heavier edge.

Lemma 3.2.2. *There is a minimal coloring that collapses* e_2.

The last case is when the mother node has only one child and no parent. In other words, the tree has only two nodes. Such trees are termed *trivial* and can be optimally colored by giving the child the color of its mother.

Notice that the invariant that exactly leaf nodes are colored remains true after any of the lemmas is used to cut/collapse edges. Thus, for any non-trivial tree, one of the two lemmas is always applicable. Since the application of a lemma reduces the number of edges, repeated application leads to a set of trivial trees. These observations lead to the algorithm given below for find a minimal coloring.

Algorithm 2. Algorithm DLC

1.   **while** $\exists$ mother node m of degree at least 2 **do**
2.   Let m have edges $e_1, \ldots, e_d$ to d children; Let $c_{e_1} \leq \ldots \leq c_{e_d}$:
3.   **if** $d > 1$ **then** cut $e_1, \ldots, e_{d-1}$
4.   **else** Let e_p be the edge from m to its parent;
5.   **if** $c_{e_p} < c_{e_1}$ **then** collapse e_1 **else** collapse e_p.
6.   **end while**;
7.   color trivial trees.

Since each iteration reduces the number of edges, the running time of the algorithm is linear in the number of edges.

3.2.3 Algorithm for Repeated Colors

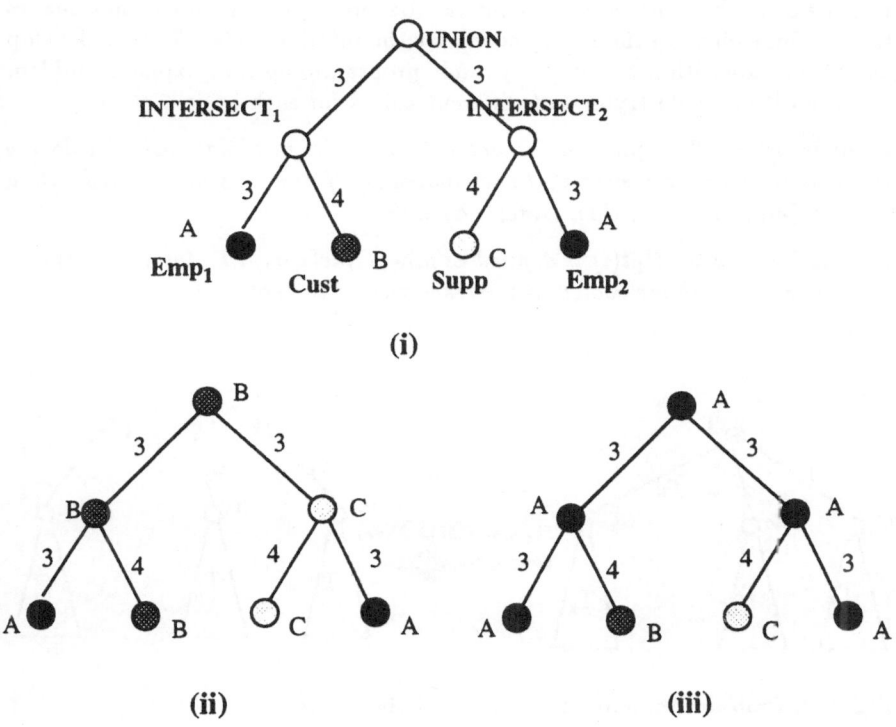

Fig. 3.4. (i) Query Tree (ii) Suboptimal DLC Coloring (cost=9) (iii) Optimal Coloring (cost=8)

The following example shows that DLC may not find the optimal coloring when colors are repeated.

Example 3.2.1. Figure 3.4(i) shows a query tree for a query that finds employees who are customers as well as suppliers. Taking the tables Supp, Cust, and Emp to be partitioned on distinct attributes, we pre-color them by colors A, B, and C respectively. We now have repeated colors and two "widely separated" leaves are both pre-colored A. The DLC algorithm finds the suboptimal coloring shown in Figure 3.4(b) since it makes a *local* choice of cutting away the A leaves. The optimal coloring shown in Figure 3.4(c) exploits the like colored leaves to achieve a lower cost.

Thus, repeated colors make it difficult to make greedy choices of colors. Brute force enumeration is undesirable since the number of colorings for c colors and n nodes is c^n.

Recall from Section 3.2.1 that a colored interior node may be split to decompose the problem into smaller subproblems that are independently solvable. Since interior nodes are all initially *uncolored*, this observation can only be exploited after coloring an interior node. A further observation that we will make is that the subproblems can be posed in a manner that makes them independent of the color chosen for the interior node. We now develop an efficient algorithm based on dynamic programming that exploits problem decomposition while trying out different colors for each node.

Definition 3.2.2. *$Optc(i, A)$ is defined to be the minimal cost of coloring the subtree rooted at i such that i is colored A. If node i is pre-colored with a color different from A, then $Optc(i, A) = \infty$.*

Definition 3.2.3. *$Opt(i)$ is defined as $\min_a Optc(i, a)$, i.e., the minimal cost of coloring the subtree rooted at i irrespective of the color of i.*

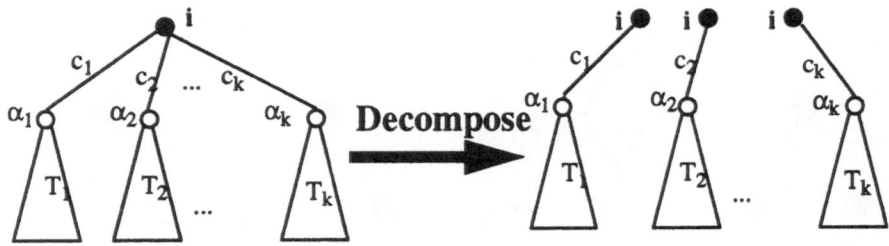

Fig. 3.5. Problem Decomposition After Coloring Node i

Consider a tree (Figure 3.5) in which root node i has children $\alpha_1, \alpha_2, \ldots, \alpha_k$. Let the edge from i to α_j have weight c_j, and let T_j be the subtree rooted at

α_j. If we fix a color for node i, we can decompose the tree into k "new" trees by splitting node i into k copies. Since the only connection between new trees was through i, they may now be colored *independently* of each other. Thus $Optc(i, A)$ is the sum of the minimal colorings for the k new trees.

Consider the jth new tree. The minimal coloring either pays for the edge (i, α_j) or it does not. If it pays for the edge, then it can do no better than using the minimal coloring for T_j, thus incurring a cost of $c_j + Opt(\alpha_j)$. If it does not pay for the edge, it can do no better than the minimal coloring that gives color A to node α_j thus incurring a cost of $Optc(\alpha_j, A)$. The next lemma follows by taking the cost of coloring the jth new tree to be the best of these cases. It provides a way of finding the *cost* of a minimal coloring.

Lemma 3.2.3. *The minimal cost $Optc(i, A)$ of coloring the subtree rooted at i such that i gets color A is*

$$Optc(i, A) = \begin{cases} \infty & i \text{ pre-colored with color other than } A \\ 0 & i \text{ a leaf, uncolored or pre-colored } A \\ \sum_{1 \le j \le k} \min[Optc(\alpha_j, A), c_j + Opt(\alpha_j)] & otherwise \end{cases}$$

Example 3.2.2. Figure 3.6 shows $Optc$ and Opt for the tree of Figure 3.4. Lemma 3.2.3 may be applied to fill up columns of these tables in a left to right manner. The first column is for the Emp_1 node that is pre-colored by color A. By the first two cases of the formula of Lemma 3.2.3, the row for color A in this column is 0 and the other two entries are ∞. The entry in the Opt table is the minimum of the column values.

NODES (POSTFIX ORDER)

		Emp_1	Cust	Intersect_1	Supp	Emp_2	Intersect_2	Union	
	A	0	∞	4	∞	0	4	8	
COLORS	B	∞	0	3	∞	∞	7	9	OPTC
	C	∞	∞	7	0	∞	3	9	
		0	0	3	0	0	3	8	OPT

Fig. 3.6. Opt and Optc Tables for Tree of Figure 3.4

Consider the last column of the table that represents entries for the Union node. This column is computed using the values in the columns for the children of the Union node, i.e., columns for Intersect_1 and Intersect_2. For example, $Optc(\text{Union}, A)$ is the sum: $\min[Optc(\text{Intersect}_1, A), 3 + Opt(\text{Intersect}_1)] + \min[Optc(\text{Intersect}_2, A), 3 + Opt(\text{Intersect}_2)]$.

If the query tree has root i, then $Opt(i)$ is the cost of the any optimal coloring. If A is a color such that $Optc(i, A) = Opt(i)$, then there must be an optimal coloring the gives color A to i. Once we know an optimal color for i, we can pick optimal colors for the children of i by applying Lemma 3.2.3 in "reverse" as follows:

Lemma 3.2.4. *If i gets color A in some minimal coloring, there exists a minimal coloring such that child α_j of i has color A if $Optc(\alpha_j, A) \leq c_j + Opt(\alpha_j)$ and any color a for which $Optc(\alpha_j, a) = Opt(\alpha_j)$ otherwise.*

Lemmas 3.2.3 and 3.2.4 lead to the following *ColorSplit* algorithm. Letting C be the set of colors used for pre-colored nodes, the algorithm has a running time of $O(n|C|)$.

Algorithm 3. Algorithm ColorSplit

1.   **for each** node i in postfix order **do** step 2
2.   **for each** color $a \in C$ **do** steps 3 and 4
3.   compute $Optc(i, a)$ using Lemma 3.2.3;
4. $Opt(i) = \min_a Optc(i, a)$
5.   Let $a \in C$ be such that $Optc(r, a) = Opt(r)$ where r is the root
6. $color(r) = a$;
7.   **for each** non-root node α_j in prefix order **do** steps 8 to 11
8.   Let i be the parent of α_j;
            Let c_j be the weight of edge between i and α_j;
9.   **if** $Optc(\alpha_j, color(i)) \leq c_j + Opt(\alpha_j)$
10.   **then** $color(\alpha_j) = color(i)$
11.   **else** $color(\alpha_j) = a \in C$ such that $Optc(\alpha_j, a) = Opt(\alpha_j)$

We further observe that *ColorSplit* does not require the input tree be such that all and only the leaf nodes are pre-colored. It finds the optimal coloring for any tree. In other words, the tree need not be pre-processed by the *Simplify* algorithm of Section 3.2.1. Having pre-colored interior nodes actually reduces the running time of *ColorSplit* since the first two cases of Lemma 3.2.3, which are simpler than the third case, may be used.

ColorSplit is a fast algorithm. While pre-processing with *Simplify* offers the possibility of reducing the running time of *ColorSplit* (by reducing the number of colors in each new tree), additional gains may not be worth the implementation effort.

3.2.4 Extensions: Using Sets of Colors

We show that the mechanism of using a *set* of colors rather than a single color to pre-color a node makes several extensions possible. Handling sets of colors does not increase the complexity of *ColorSplit*. The intuitive reason is that any pre-coloring constrains the search space and thus can only reduce the running time of the algorithm.

Pre-coloring with a set of nodes serves to restrict the choices of colors that the *ColorSplit* algorithm may make for a node. This restriction is implemented by the formula given in Lemma 3.2.3 which may be modified as shown below.

Lemma 3.2.5 (Modified Lemma 3.2.3). *The minimal cost $Optc(i, A)$ of coloring the subtree rooted at i such that i gets color A is given by*

$$Optc(i, A) = \begin{cases} \infty & A \text{ is not in set of pre-colors for } i \\ 0 & i \text{ a leaf, uncolored or has } A \text{ as pre-color} \\ \sum_{1 \leq j \leq k} \min[Optc(\alpha_j, A), c_j + Opt(\alpha_j)] & otherwise \end{cases}$$

This is the only modification needed for *ColorSplit* to work with a set of pre-colors. The modified algorithm finds the optimal in $O(n|C|)$ running time. Notice that using a set of pre-colors does not change the worst case running time of the algorithm since any pre-coloring (set or single color) reduces the running time of the algorithm by simplifying the computation of $Optc$.

Access Methods:. Typically, the columns needed from a table may be accessed in several alternate ways. For example if a table is replicated then any copy may be accessed. Further, an index provides a copy of the indexing columns as well as permits access to the remaining columns. Each access method may potentially provide a different partitioning. We may model this situation by associating a set of colors with each base table node, one color per partitioning. We observe that each access method may have a different cost in addition to delivering a different partitioning. Such interactions between the cost of computation and communication are handled in Section 3.3.

Compound Attributes:. Thus far we have considered attribute sensitive operators such as joins and groupings to have a single color. When such operators are based on compound attributes, additional opportunities for optimization arise that may be expressed by sets of pre-colors.

Example 3.2.3. Given the tables Emp(emp#, dep#, city) and Dep(dep#, city), the following query finds employees who live in the same city as the the location of their department.

Select e **From** Emp e, Dep d
Where e.dep# = d.dep# **and** e.city = d.city
Since a join operator has to be partitioned on the join column, the required partitioning depends on the predicate chosen to be the join predicate. In Figure 3.7, the first query tree uses the join predicate on **dep#** and requires the Emp table to be repartitioned. The second uses the join predicate on city and requires Dep to be repartitioned. The optimization opportunities provided by join predicates may be modeled by pre-coloring the join node by a set of two colors {dep#, city}. We observe that choice of the join predicate may impact the cost of the join-method. Such interactions between the cost of computation and communication are postponed to Section 3.3.

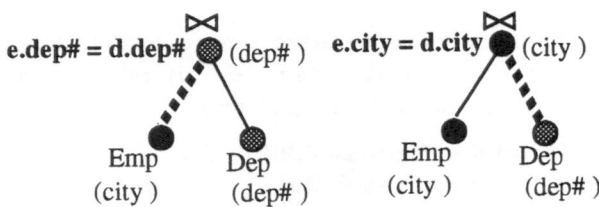

Fig. 3.7. Interaction of Repartitioning with Join Predicates

Similar observations apply to other attribute sensitive operators. Given a grouping of employees by department and city, we pre-color the GROUPBY operator by {dep#, city}. A partitioning guarantees that tuples that agree on the partitioning attribute(s) are assigned to the same site. Given some set of attributes X, a partitioning on any non-empty subset of X is also a partitioning on X. The most general way of modeling this situation is by pre-coloring an attribute sensitive operator that has compound attribute X by a set colors, one color for each non-empty subset of X.

Partitioning Functions:. Suppose two base tables are partitioned on the same attribute A using different partitioning functions (We consider two attributes to be the "same" attribute w.r.t. a query if they are equated by an equality predicate.) For example, one table may be hash partitioned on A and the other range partitioned. We will fix this situation by giving distinct colors (say B_1 and B_2) to the two tables. Any attribute sensitive operator that needs a partitioning on A could use either of the two partitions and will therefore be given the set of colors $\{B_1, B_2\}$.

3.3 Model for Methods and Physical Properties

We have so far been concerned with communication costs incurred by repartitioning and have blithely considered the cost of an operator to be independent of the partitioning attribute.

Several alternate *strategies*, each with a different cost, may be available for an operator. The following example shows that the cost of an operator depends on the chosen strategy as well as several physical properties of data. The partitioning attribute is simply one of these physical properties.

Example 3.3.1. Given the schema Emp(emp#, salary, dep#, city) and Dep(dep#, city), the following query finds the average salaries of employees grouped by city for those employees who live in the same city as the the location of their department.

Select e.city, **avg**(e.salary)
From Emp e, Dep d
Where e.dep# = d.dep# **and** e.city = d.city
Group by e.city;

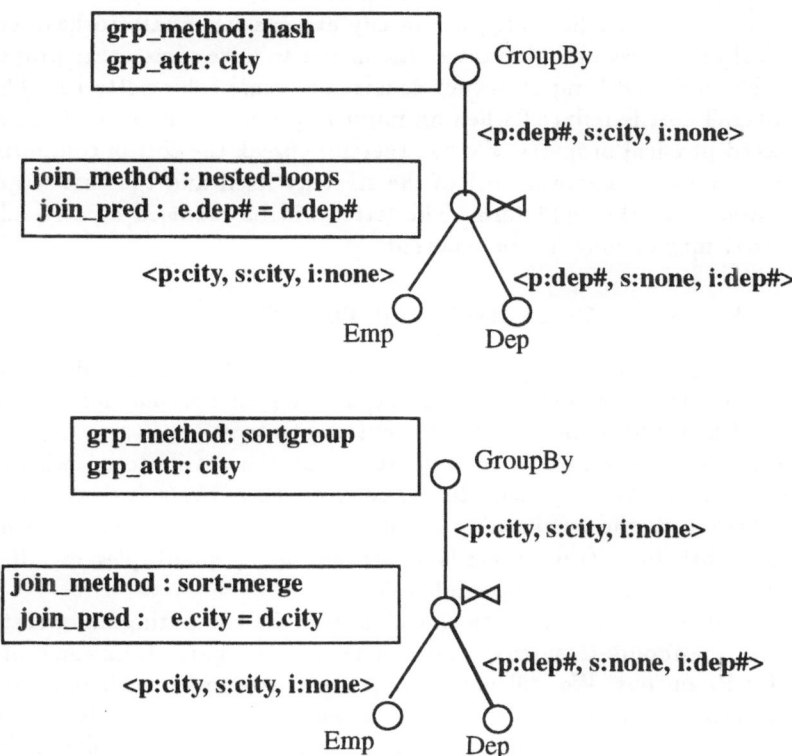

Fig. 3.8. Annotated Query Trees

Suppose Emp is partitioned by city and each partition is stored in sorted order by city. Suppose Dep is partitioned by dep# and each partition has an index on dep#. Figure 3.8 shows two query trees. The computation of Avg is assumed to be combined with GroupBy. The first query tree uses the join predicate on dep# and repartitions the Emp table. Due to the availability of an index on Dep, a nested-loops IndexJoin!nested-loops strategy may be the cheapest for joining each partition of Emp (outer) with its corresponding partition of Dep (inner). The grouping operator is implemented by a hash-grouping strategy.

The second query tree uses the join predicate on city and repartitions the Dep table. Since each partition of Emp is pre-sorted, it may be cheapest to use a sort-merge join for joining corresponding partitions. Since the output of merge join is pre-sorted in addition to being pre-partitioned on the city, the grouping operator uses a sort-grouping strategy.

The example illustrates several points. Firstly, while partitioning impacts communication costs, other physical properties (sort-order and   indexes) impact operator cost. We will generalize the notion of a color to capture *all* physical properties. Secondly, a strategy expects its inputs to have certain physical properties and guarantees its output to have some other properties. We will specify such input-output constraints using color patterns. Thirdly, the overall cost is reduced when an input to a strategy happens to have the expected physical property. We will therefore break the cost of computing an operator into the intrinsic cost of the strategy itself and the cost of getting the inputs into the right form. The latter will be modeled as a re-coloring cost that may or may not be incurred.

3.3.1 Annotated Query Trees and Their Cost

We now allow a query tree to have annotations. Each interior node of a query tree is annotated by a strategy, an output color, and a color for each input. The leaf nodes have an output color but no strategy.

We have so far used a color to represent the attribute on which data is partitioned. We now generalize a color to be a *triple* $\langle p : a_1, s : a_2, i : a_3 \rangle$ where a_1 is the partitioning attribute, a_2 the sort attribute and a_3 the indexing attribute (this is easily generalizable to quadruples etc. if more physical properties are to be modeled).

A strategy specifies a particular algorithm for computing an operator. It requires the inputs to satisfy some constraints and guarantees some properties for its output. We will use *color patterns* to specify such input-output constraints. A constraint has the form $Input_1, \ldots, Input_k \rightarrow Output$, where $Input_j$ and $Output$ are color patterns. A color pattern is similar in syntax to a color but allows the use of variables and wild-cards. Table 3.1 shows examples of input-output constraints for several strategies.

If some input is not colored as required, a re-coloring is needed. Re-coloring requires repartitioning, sorting, or building an index.

Example 3.3.2. The Emp table of Example 3.3.1 (Figure 3.8) has the output color $\langle p : \mathrm{city}, s : \mathrm{city}, i : \mathrm{none} \rangle$ while Dep has $\langle p : \mathrm{dep\#}, s : \mathrm{none}, i : \mathrm{dep\#} \rangle$. In the first query tree of Figure 3.8, the join uses the nested-loops strategy and its output has the color $\langle p : \mathrm{dep\#}, s : \mathrm{city}, i : \mathrm{none} \rangle$. From the first row of Table 3.1, this implies that the color of input1 (Emp) should be $\langle p : \mathrm{dep\#}, s : \mathrm{city}, i : * \rangle$ and that of input2 (Dep) should be $\langle p : \mathrm{dep\#}, s : *, i : \mathrm{dep\#} \rangle$. The color of Dep matches the requirements but that of Emp does not.

Our goal is to devise an abstract cost model that is compatible with classical cost models. Such classical models typically consists of two parts: (a)

Strategy	Output	Input1	Input2
Nested-Loops Join[†]	$\langle p:X, s:Y, i:none\rangle$	$\langle p:X, s:Y, i:*\rangle$	$\langle p:X, s:*, i:X\rangle$
Sort-Merge Join[†]	$\langle p:X, s:X, i:none\rangle$	$\langle p:X, s:X, i:*\rangle$	$\langle p:X, s:X, i:*\rangle$
Hybrid-Hash Join[†]	$\langle p:X, s:Y, i:none\rangle$	$\langle p:X, s:Y, i:*\rangle$	$\langle p:X, s:*, i:*\rangle$
Hash Grouping[+]	$\langle p:X, s:none, i:none\rangle$	$\langle p:X, s:*, i:*\rangle$	
Sort Grouping[+]	$\langle p:X, s:X, i:none\rangle$	$\langle p:X, s:X, i:*\rangle$	
Hash Intersect	$\langle p:X, s:none, i:none\rangle$	$\langle p:X, s:*, i:*\rangle$	$\langle p:X, s:*, i:*\rangle$

[†]Additional requirement: Join predicate on X
[+]Additional requirement: X is a grouping attribute

Table 3.1. Examples of Input-Output Constraints

estimation of statistics (such as size, number of unique values in columns) for intermediate results; and, (b) estimation of cost of an operator given statistics and physical properties of operands. Our goal is not to provide new formulas but to provide abstractions that make it possible to reason with formulas provided by existing models in a more general manner.

Definition 3.3.1. R^s *is the set of statistics for table R. R^s depends only on the contents of table R, not on how it is physically stored.*

Definition 3.3.2. $recolor(R^s, c_{old}, c_{new})$ *is the cost of re-coloring table R from c_{old} to c_{new}.*

Definition 3.3.3. $inpCol(s, A, j)$ *is the color pattern needed by strategy s for input j for the output to be of color pattern A.*

Example 3.3.3. The color required for the first input of the nested-loops join in the first query tree of Figure 3.8 is $c_{new} = \langle p : \mathbf{dep\#}, s : \mathbf{city}, i : *\rangle$. Since the output color (call it c_{old}) of *Emp* differs in partitioning attribute, $recolor(R, c_{old}, c_{new})$ is the cost of repartitioning Emp on the city attribute.

The cost of an annotated query tree is the sum of the costs of all operators. The cost of an operator consists of re-coloring the inputs to have colors needed by the chosen strategy plus the cost of the strategy itself (StrategyCost). Suppose the root of tree T uses strategy s and has output color a. Let $c'_j = inpCol(s, a, j)$, the color required by strategy s for the j'th input. Let T have k immediate subtrees $T_1, \ldots, T_k$ such that T_j produces table R_j with color c_j.

$$Cost(T) = StrategyCost(s, R_1^s, \ldots, R_k^s) + \sum_{j=1}^{k} recolor(R_j^s, c_j, c'_j) + \sum_{j=1}^{k} Cost(T_j)$$

If T is a leaf, we take its cost as zero since we count the cost of accessing operands as part of the cost of a strategy. Since the output of a query is always shipped to an application, the root of any query tree will be a unary operator that achieves the shipping. By convention, we will omit showing this operator[2].

Observe that *no restriction* is placed on the *form* of the *StrategyCost()* or *recolor()* functions. This allows, for example, non-linear terms such as logarithms, product and division that do occur in the classical System R [SAC+79] cost model.

3.4 Extension of ColorSplit for Methods and Physical Properties

We will now develop an extension of *ColorSplit* that given a tree with colors for the leaf nodes finds a minimal-cost strategy as well as input and output colors for each interior node.

Definition 3.4.1. *$Optc(i, A)$ is defined to be the minimal cost of the subtree rooted at node i such that i has output color A. $OptcStrategy(i, A)$ is defined to be the strategy that achieves this minimal value (pick any one strategy if several are minimal).*

For a leaf node i, $Optc(i, A) = 0$ if i is pre-colored with a color compatible with A and ∞ otherwise. We will treat $OptcStrategy(i, A)$ as undefined for leaf nodes.

Definition 3.4.2. *$Strategies(i, A)$ is the set of strategies applicable to the operator represented by node i and whose input-output constraint permits A as an output color.*

The following is a generalization of Lemma 3.2.3. Let node i have children $\alpha_1, \ldots, \alpha_k$. Suppose the subtree rooted at α_j computes table R_j as its output. The minimum cost of the tree rooted at i such that i has output color A is obtained by trying out all strategies capable of producing output color A. The lemma shows that for any such strategy s, the lowest cost is achieved by *individually* minimizing the cost of each input.

Lemma 3.4.1. *For a leaf node i, $Optc(i, A)$ is 0 if i has a color compatible with A and ∞ otherwise. For non-leaf node i, $Optc(i, A)$ obeys the following recurrence.*

$Optc(i, A) = \min_{s \in S}[StrategyCost(s, R_1^s, \ldots, R_k^s) +$
$\qquad\qquad \sum_{j=1}^{k} \min_{c \in C}[Optc(\alpha_j, c) + recolor(R_j^s, c, inpCol(s, A, j))]]$
where $S = Strategies(i, A)$

$OptcStrategy(i, A)$ is some strategy for which the minima is achieved.

---

[2] Consider a query that simply scans a table. It will have a query tree consisting of a Ship with Scan as the only child. Observe that the cost of scanning data is counted as part of Ship.

Using the lemma, the following algorithm computes *Optc* and *OptcStrategy* by a bottom-up followed by a subsequent top-down pass that extracts optimal colors and strategies.

Algorithm 4. Algorithm ExtendedColorSplit
1. **for each** node i in postfix order **do** step 2
2.   for each color $a \in C$
       Use Lemma 3.4.1 to compute $Optc(i, a)$ and $OptcStrategy(i, a)$
3. Let r be the root and a a color
   s.t. $Optc(r, a) \leq Optc(r, c)$ for all colors $c \in C$
4. Optimal color for r is a and optimal strategy is $OptcStrategy(r, a)$
5. **for each** non-root node in prefix order **do** step 6
6.   compute optimal colors and strategies by top-down
       pass applying Lemma 3.4.1 in reverse.

The algorithm has a worst-case running time of $nS|C|^2$ where S is the number of strategies, $|C|$ the number of allowable colors and n the number of nodes in the tree.

Since n and S are typically small, the running time of the algorithm is dependent on $|C|$. $|C|$ can become large when we permit the extensions discussed in section 3.2.4. The magnitude of $|C|$ may be kept small by observing (1) no strategy yields an output relation with an index. Thus only 2 components of the triple for colors are relevant for interior nodes (2) only colors that might be useful to subsequent operator need to be considered.

3.5 Model with Join Ordering

We now show an example of how repartitioning costs interact with the order of joins.

Example 3.5.1. Suppose that the tables Emp(emp#, city), EmpSkills(emp#, skill#), and Skills(skill#, skilltype) are partitioned by the underlined attributes. The following query finds employees who live in Palo Alto and have analytical skills.
Select e from Emp e, EmpSkills es, Skills s
Where   e.emp# = es.emp# and es.skill# = s.skill# and
        s.skilltype = Analytical and e.city = Palo Alto
Figure 3.9(i) and (ii) shows two alternate query trees. The trees use different join orders and incur different repartitioning costs. If "s.skilltype = analytical" is a highly selective predicate, the second tree may achieve a low cost due to the small size of the intermediate table (Skills ⋈ EmpSkills). However, the first tree avoids the cost of repartitioning the possibly very large EmpSkills table. Thus repartitioning cost impacts the ordering of joins. Figure 3.9(iii) illustrates the details of the strategy annotations for join operations.

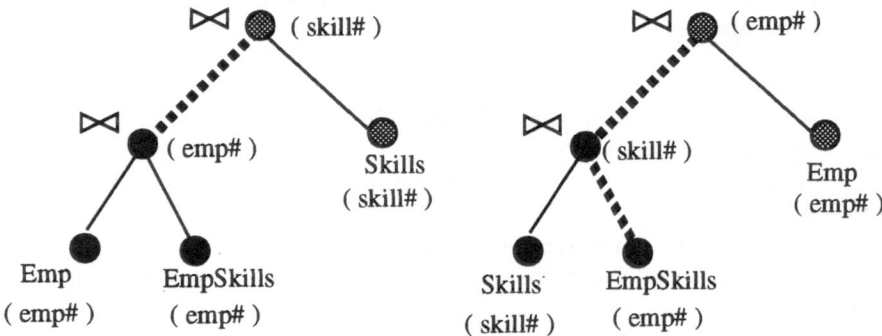

Fig. 3.9. Interaction of Repartitioning with Order of Joins

Commercially adopted solutions to join ordering are typically variations of the System R algorithm [SAC+79]. Our goal is to combine the basic ideas from this algorithm with the *ColorSplit* algorithm. We will start by developing an abstraction of some aspects of the System R style dynamic programming. This will us to understand and analyze the basic ideas while ignoring many details of the actual algorithm.

3.5.1 Join Ordering Without Physical Properties

Definition 3.5.1. *A join tree is an annotated query tree in which all interior nodes represent 2-way join operations and leaves represent tables.*

Since join operations are associative and commutative, they may be performed in any order. Given a SPJ query on tables $T_1, \ldots, T_n$, the *join ordering problem* is to find a minimal cost join tree for computing the query. A join tree fixes the *order* of joins in addition to the *strategy* for each join. We will use a nested list notation to represent join trees. For example, the tree of figure 3.9(iii) may be represented as $[s_2, [s_1, \text{Skills}, \text{EmpSkills}], \text{Emp}]$

For simplicity, we first consider the case when re-coloring has zero cost. In other words, physical properties do not make a difference to cost and we have:

$$Cost(T) = \begin{cases} 0 & \text{if } T \text{ is a leaf} \\ StrategyCost(s, R_l^s, R_r^s) + \\ Cost(T_l) + Cost(t_r) & \text{if } T = [s, T_l, T_r] \end{cases}$$

The following lemma follows from the structure of the cost formula and implies that any subtree of an optimal query tree must be an optimal query tree for the corresponding sub-query.

Lemma 3.5.1. *If $OptPlan(Q) = [s, T_l, T_r]$ and $Q = Q_l \cup Q_r$ where T_l computes the sub-query over Q_l and T_r over Q_r, then $OptPlan(Q_l) = T_l$ and $OptPlan(Q_r) = T_r$*

This lemma leads to the following dynamic programming algorithm:

Algorithm 5. Algorithm JO (Join Ordering)
Input: SPJ query on tables $T = \{T_1, \ldots, T_n\}$
Output: Optimal join tree.
1. **for** $i = 1$ to n **do** $OptPlan(\{T_i\}) = T_i$
2. **for** $i = 2$ to n **do** step 3
3.   **for each** $Q \subseteq T$ s.t. $|Q| = i$ **do** steps 4 and 5
4. $bestCost = \infty$
5.   **for each** $Q_l \neq \emptyset$, $Q_r \neq \emptyset$ s.t. $Q = Q_l \cup Q_r$ **do** steps 6 and 7
6   Let R_l^s, R_r^s be statistics for tables computed by queries Q_l, Q_r
7.   **for each** join strategy s **do** steps 8 to 11
8.   **if** $StrategyCost(s, R_l^s, R_r^s) < bestCost$ **then**
9. $bestCost = StrategyCost(s, R_l^s, R_r^s)$
10. $OptPlan(Q) = [s, OptPlan(Q_l), OptPlan(Q_r)]$
11.   **end if**

The algorithm has a running time of $O(3^n)$. Since plans for all subsets of Q are cached, and a plan for i tables has storage cost proportional to i, the space requirements of the algorithm are $O(n2^n)$. A brute force enumeration of all trees would run in $O(2n!/n!)$ time but require only $O(n)$ space (for 1 plan).

Often systems choose a restricted class of shapes of join trees. A popular restriction is left-deep trees that require the left child of any interior node to be a leaf. This cuts the number of trees to $n!$ and the algorithm runs in $O(n2^n)$ time.

3.5.2 Join Ordering with Physical Properties

Suppose strategy s requires input colors c_l' and c_r'. Suppose sub-plan (subtree) T_l produces table R_l with color c_l (R_r and c_r for sub-plan T_r).

$$
Cost(T) = \begin{cases}
0 & \text{if } T \text{ is a leaf} \\
\begin{aligned}
&recolor(R_l^s, c_l, c_l') + \\
&recolor(R_r^s, c_r, c_r') + \\
&StrategyCost(s, R_l^s, R_r^s) + \\
&Cost(T_l) + Cost(T_r)
\end{aligned} & \text{if } T = [s, T_l, T_r]
\end{cases}
$$

Let $Optc(Q, A)$ be the cost of an optimal join tree for the set of tables Q such that the output has physical property A.

Lemma 3.5.2. *$Optc(Q, a)$ obeys the following recurrence:*

$Optc(Q, a) =$
$min_{Q_l, Q_r}[min_{s \in S}[StrategyCost(s, Q_l, Q_r)$
$\qquad\qquad + min_{a \in C}[Optc(Q_l, a) + recolor(Q_l^s, a, inpCol(s, a, 1))]$
$\qquad\qquad + min_{a \in C}[Optc(Q_r, a) + recolor(Q_r^s, a, inpCol(s, a, 2))]]]]$

where Q_l and Q_r are all sets such that $Q = Q_l \cup Q_r$, $Q_l \neq \emptyset$, $Q_r \neq \emptyset$ and S is the set of strategies that produce property a.

Algorithm 6. Algorithm *JOP* (Join Ordering With Physical Properties)

Input: An SPJ query on tables $T = \{T_1, \ldots, T_n\}$
Output: An optimal join tree.

1. **for** $i = 1$ to n **do** step 2

2. $\quad Optc(T_i, a) = \begin{cases} 0 & T_i \text{ has access method with physical property } a \\ \infty & \text{otherwise} \end{cases}$

3. **for** $i = 2$ to n **do** step 4
4. $\quad$ **for each** $Q \subseteq T$ s.t. $|Q| = i$ **do** steps 5 and 6
5. $\qquad Optc(Q, a) = \infty$ for each physical property $a \in C$
6. $\qquad$ **for each** $Q_l \neq \emptyset$, $Q_r \neq \emptyset$ s.t. $Q = Q_l \cup Q_r$ **do** steps 7 and 8
7. $\qquad\quad$ Let R_l^s, R_r^s be statistics for tables computed by queries Q_l, Q_r
8. $\qquad\quad$ **for each** physical property $a \in C$ **do** step 9
9. $\qquad\qquad$ **for each strategy** s **that can produce property** a
$\qquad\qquad$ **do** steps 10 and 11
10. $\qquad\qquad\quad$ Let $scost = StrategyCost(s, R_l^s, R_r^s)$,
$\qquad\qquad\qquad a_l' = inpCol(s, a, 1)$ and $a_r' = inpCol(s, a, 2)$
11. $\qquad\qquad\quad$ **for each** physical property $a_l \in C, a_r \in C$
$\qquad\qquad\qquad$ **do** steps 12 to 16
12. $\qquad\qquad\qquad$ Let $newcost = scost + Optc(Q_l, a_l) + recolor(R_l^s, a_l, a_l')$
$\qquad\qquad\qquad\qquad + Optc(Q_r, a_r) + recolor(R_r^s, a_r, a_r')$
13. $\qquad\qquad\qquad$ **if** $newcost < Optc(Q, a)$ **then**
14. $\qquad\qquad\qquad\quad Optc(Q, a) = newcost$
15. $\qquad\qquad\qquad\quad OptPlan(Q, a) = [s, OptPlan(Q_l, a_l), OptPlan(Q_r, a_r)]$
16. $\qquad\qquad\qquad$ **end if**
17. **return** $Min_{a \in C} OptPlan(T, a)$

A complex query may be decomposed into SPJ queries connected by other operators(Figure 3.10). We remark that it is possible to integrate the *JOP* and *ExtendedColorSplit* algorithms in a straightforward manner to produce an optimal annotated query tree. The tree is optimal with respect to all allowed orderings within SPJ boxes and all possible annotations of nodes.

3.6 Usage of Algorithms

There are several ways in which the algorithms developed in this chapter may be used. One possibility is to use *ExtendedColorSplit* as a post-pass

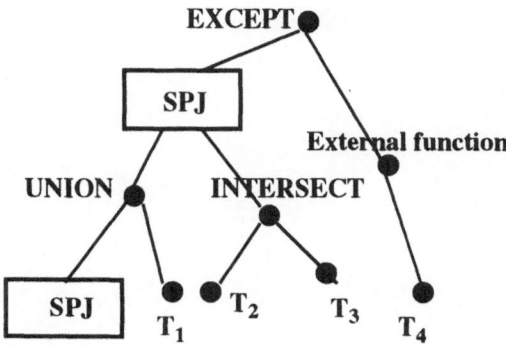

Fig. 3.10. Decomposition of a Complex Query

to a conventional optimizer. This has two advantages. First, no modifications is required to existing optimizers. Secondly, *ExtendedColorSplit* runs in polynomial time. The disadvantage is that the query trees will have optimal annotations given the join orders produced by the conventional optimizer. The second possibility is to produce optimal join order as well as annotation by using the integration of the *JOP* and *ExtendedColorSplit* as a replacement for a conventional optimizer.

4. Scheduling Pipelined Parallelism

In this chapter[1], we focus on the problem of scheduling a pipelined operator tree, which is an operator tree in which all edges are pipelining edges. Pipelined parallelism permits all operators in such a tree to run concurrently. Scheduling such trees poses a parallelism-communication trade-off. A producer and a consumer operator must either communicate data across processors to benefit from and run on distinct processors, or they must share a processor but save communication.

We will measure the quality of scheduling algorithms by their *performance ratio* [GJ79] which is the ratio of the response time of the generated schedule to that of the optimal. Our goal is to devise algorithms that are near-optimal in the sense that the average performance ratio should be close to 1 and the worst performance ratio should be a small constant.

We start by defining the problem more precisely. We then develop and analyze several algorithms followed by an experimental comparison.

4.1 Problem Definition

Definition 4.1.1. *Given p processors and an operator tree $T = (V, E)$, a schedule is a partition of V, the set of nodes, into p sets $F_1, \ldots, F_p$ with set F_k allocated to processor k.*

The cost of executing F_k is the cost of executing all nodes in F_k plus the cost for communicating with nodes on other processors. It is thus the sum of the weights of all nodes in F_k and the weights of all edges that connect a node within F_k to a node outside. For convenience, we define $c_{ij} = 0$ if there is no edge from i to j.

Definition 4.1.2. *The load L_k on processor k is $\sum_{i \in F_k}[t_i + \sum_{j \notin F_k} c_{ij}]$.*

The response time, L, of a schedule may be derived by observing that pipelining constraints force all operators in a pipeline to start simultaneously

---

[1] Parts of this chapter have been published in the two papers
W. Hasan and R. Motwani: *Optimization Algorithms for Exploiting the Parallelism-Communication Tradeoff in Pipelined Parallelism, VLDB94*
C. Chekuri, W. Hasan and R. Motwani: *Scheduling Problems in Parallel Query Optimization, PODS95*

(time 0) and terminate simultaneously at time L. Fast operators are forced to "stretch" over a longer time period by the slow operators. Suppose operator i is allocated to processor k and uses fraction f_i of the processor. The pipelining constraint is then:

$$f_i = \frac{1}{L}[t_i + \sum_{j \notin F_k} c_{ij}] \quad \text{for all operators } i \in V \tag{4.1}$$

The utilization of a processor is the sum of utilizations of the operators executing on it. Since at least one processor must be saturated (otherwise the pipeline would speed up):

$$\max_{1 \le k \le p} [\sum_{i \in F_k} f_i] = 1$$

$$\Rightarrow \quad L = \max_{1 \le k \le p} [\sum_{i \in F_k} [t_i + \sum_{j \notin F_k} c_{ij}]] = \max_{1 \le k \le p} L_k \quad \text{using equation (4.1)}$$

Example 4.1.1. Figure 4.1(a) shows a schedule by encircling the sets F_k. The cost of each set is underlined. For example {PROBE(h1)} costs 8 by adding up its node weight (7) and the weight of the edge (1) connecting it to its child. Observe that we show edges as undirected since the parallel constraint represented by pipelining edges is symmetric. Figure 4.1(b) shows a Gantt chart of the execution specified by the schedule. The fraction of the processor used by each operator in shown in parenthesis.

The pipelined operator tree scheduling (POT) problem may now be stated as follows:

Input: Operator Tree $T = (V, E)$ with positive real weights t_i for each
       node $i \in V$ and c_{ij} for each edge $(i, j) \in E$; number of processors p
Output: A schedule with minimal response time i.e., a partition of V into
       $F_1, \ldots, F_p$ that minimizes $\max_{1 \le l \le p} \sum_{i \in F_l} [t_i + \sum_{j \notin F_l} c_{ij}]$.

Definition 4.1.3. *If F is a set of operators, cost(F) is the load on a processor that computes F.*

$$cost(F) = \sum_{i \in F} [t_i + \sum_{j \notin F} c_{ij}]$$

Since the special case in which all edge weights are zero is *multiprocessor scheduling* [GJ79, GLLK79], POT is NP-hard. Since the number of ways of partitioning n elements into k disjoint non-empty sets is $\left\{ {n \atop k} \right\}$ (which denotes Stirling numbers of the second kind) [Knu73], the number of distinct schedules for a tree with n nodes on p processors is $\sum_{1 \le k \le p} \left\{ {n \atop k} \right\}$. This number is about 1.2×10^5 for $n = p = 10$ and 5.0×10^{13} for $n = p = 20$, thus ruling out enumerative approaches to the problem.

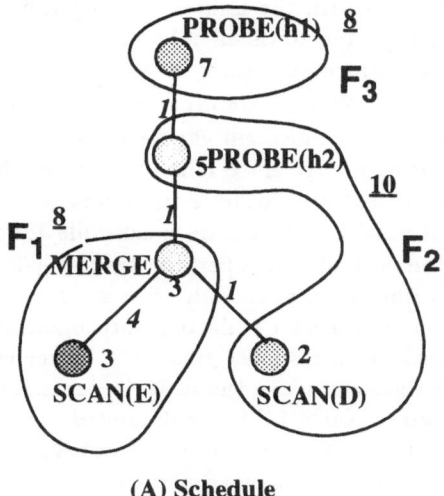

(A) Schedule

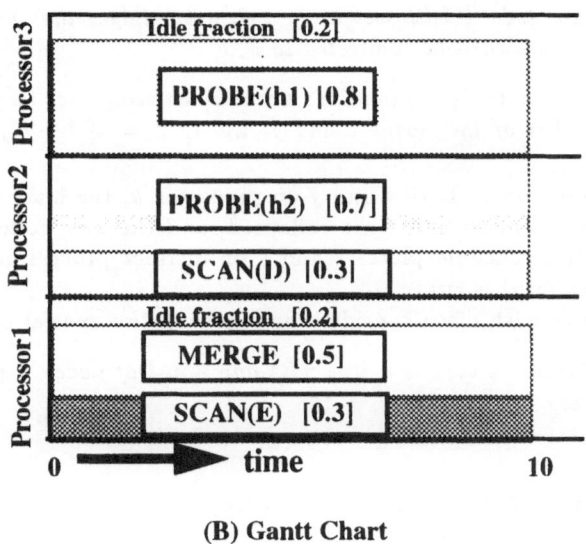

(B) Gantt Chart

Fig. 4.1. A Pipelined Schedule and Its Execution

A natural question is whether multiprocessor scheduling algorithms such as *LPT* may be adapted for POT. Multiprocessor scheduling is the problem of scheduling independent jobs with known running times on a set of processors. *LPT* assigns the job with the largest running time to the least loaded processor, repeating this step until all jobs are assigned. For p processors, *LPT* has a worst case performance ratio of $\frac{4}{3} - \frac{1}{3p}$ [Gra69].

LPT may be applied to POT by simply using the *cost* of each node (i.e. the node weight plus weights of all incident edges) as its running time. This *Naive LPT* algorithm performs poorly since it is unaware of the tradeoff between parallelism and communication. Consider two operators each of weight t connected by an edge of weight c. To obtain a schedule for 2 processors, *Naive LPT* will consider the cost of each operator to be $t + c$ and place them on separate processors resulting in a schedule with a response time of $t + c$. *LPT* never saves communication cost by placing both operators on a single processor which would achieve a response time of $2t$. Since cheap operators and expensive communication can make the ratio $\frac{t+c}{2t}$ arbitrarily large, the worst case performance ratio of Naive LPT is unbounded.

Our algorithms will use the operations of cutting and collapsing edges that correspond to decisions to place adjacent nodes on the same or different processors.

Definition 4.1.4. *Collapse(i, j) modifies a tree by replacing nodes i and j by a single new node i' with weight $t_{i'} = t_i + t_j$. Edges that were connected to either i or j are instead connected to i'.*

Definition 4.1.5. *Cut(i, j) modifies a tree by deleting edge (i, j) and adding its weight to that of the nodes i and j, i.e. $t_i^{new} = t_i^{old} + c_{ij}$ and $t_j^{new} = t_j^{old} + c_{ij}$.*

If a schedule places both i and j on processor k, the load on all processors is invariant when i and j are collapsed, and the new node is placed on processor k. If a schedule places i and j on distinct processors, the load is invariant when (i, j) is cut.

Our analysis with often consider the following two special cases.

Definition 4.1.6. *A star is a tree with one non-leaf node. A path is a tree with two leaves.*

4.2 Identifying Worthless Parallelism

In this section we investigate the tradeoff between parallelism and communication cost and develop the *GreedyChase* algorithm that "chases" down and removes parallelism that is "worthless" irrespective of the number of processors.

We start by characterizing *worthless edges* whose communication overhead is relatively high enough to exceed any benefits from parallelism. We the identify a class of trees that we call *monotone*. Such trees have no worthless parallelism in the sense that maximal use of parallelism is in fact optimal. We show that repeatedly collapsing worthless edges results in a monotone tree. Finally, we provide lower bounds on schedules for monotone trees.

4.2.1 Worthless Edges and Monotone Trees

In Figure 4.1, the cost incurred by MERGE in communicating with SCAN(E) is 4 seconds which exceeds the cost of SCAN(E) itself. It is thus always better for the processor executing MERGE to execute SCAN(E) locally rather than communicate with it. We now generalize this observation.

Definition 4.2.1. *An edge e_{ij} is* worthless *if and only if* $(c_{ij} \geq t_i + \sum_{k \neq j} c_{ik})$ *or* $(c_{ij} \geq t_j + \sum_{k \neq i} c_{jk})$.
The following theorem shows that our definition of worthless indeed captures edges whose high communication cost offsets the advantage of parallel execution.

Theorem 4.2.1. *Given p processors and an operator tree T with worthless edge (i,j), there exists an optimal schedule of T for p processors in which nodes i and j are assigned to the same processor.*

Proof. We prove the theorem by showing that given a worthless edge (i,j) and an optimal schedule S, we can generate another schedule S' (for the same number of processors) with no higher response time in which (i,j) is collapsed.

Let F_p and F_q be the sets of nodes assigned to processors p and q in S such that $i \in F_p$ and $j \in F_q$. Since (i,j) is worthless, without loss of generality we may assume

$$c_{ij} \geq t_j + \sum_{k \neq i} c_{jk} \tag{4.2}$$

We show S' to consist of S modified by moving j from q to p. This move changes the loads only on p and q and we show that neither load can increase.

Moving j onto processor p increases the load on p by *at most* $[t_j + \sum_{k \in (V - F_p)} c_{jk}] - c_{ij}$, since p saves the cost of the edge between i and j, but incurs the additional cost of j as well as j communicating with nodes other than those assigned to p. Observing that $\sum_{k \in (V - F_p)} c_{jk} \leq \sum_{k \neq i} c_{jk}$, Equation 4.2 shows this increase cannot be positive.

Removing j from processor q increases the load on q by $-c_{ij} - t_j + \sum_{k \in F_q} c_{jk}$, since q saves the cost of j, and j communicating with i, but must now incur the cost of the remaining nodes of F_q communicating with j. Observing that $\sum_{k \in F_q} c_{jk} \leq \sum_{k \neq i} c_{jk}$, Equation 4.2 shows this increase cannot be positive.

Definition 4.2.2. *An operator tree is* monotone *if and only if any connected set of nodes, X, has a lower cost than any connected superset, Y, i.e., if $X \subset Y$ then $cost(X) < cost(Y)$.*

We now establish an important connection between worthless edges and monotone trees. The following theorem allows us to transform *any* tree into a monotone tree by collapsing all worthless edges. More importantly, we can schedule the monotone tree rather than the original tree. This follows since collapsing worthless edges does not sacrifice optimality (Theorem 4.2.1) and the schedule for the original tree can be recovered from the schedule for the transformed tree.

Theorem 4.2.2. *A tree is monotone if and only if it has no worthless edges.*

Proof. [WORTHLESS EDGE IMPLIES NON-MONOTONICITY]
Assume edge (i, j) is a worthless edge. Without loss of generality, we assume

$$c_{ij} \geq t_j + \sum_{k \neq i} c_{jk} \tag{4.3}$$

We show $cost(\{i\}) \geq cost(\{i, j\})$ and hence the tree is not monotone.

$$
\begin{aligned}
cost(\{i\}) &= t_i + \sum_k c_{ik} \\
&= t_i + c_{ij} + \sum_{k \neq j} c_{ik} \\
&\geq t_i + (t_j + \sum_{k \neq i} c_{ij}) + \sum_{k \neq j} c_{ik} \quad \text{by Equation 4.3} \\
&= cost(\{i, j\})
\end{aligned}
$$

[NON-MONOTONICITY IMPLIES WORTHLESS EDGE]
If a tree is not monotone, there must be connected sets X and Y such that $X \subset Y$ with $cost(X) \geq cost(Y)$. Since X and Y are both connected sets, it must be possible to arrange the nodes in $Y - X$ in a sequence $v_1, \ldots, v_m$ such that Y can be created from X by adding these nodes one by one and guaranteeing a connected set at all steps. That is, we progress through sets $F_0, F_1, \ldots, F_m$ with $F_i = F_0 \cup \{v_1, \ldots, v_i\}$ being a connected set and with $F_0 = X$ and $F_m = Y$. Since $cost(F_0) \geq cost(F_m)$, there must be some vertex v_α, such that $cost(F_{\alpha-1}) \geq cost(F_\alpha)$. Since both $F_{\alpha-1}$ and F_α are connected but acyclic sets, v_α is connected to exactly one node in $F_{\alpha-1}$. Call that node β.

$$cost(F_\alpha) = cost(F_{\alpha-1}) + t_\alpha - c_{\alpha\beta} + \sum_{j \neq \beta} c_{\alpha j}$$

Using $cost(F_{\alpha-1}) \geq cost(F_\alpha)$, we can conclude $t_\alpha + \sum_{j \neq \beta} c_{\alpha j} \leq c_{\alpha\beta}$ which proves (α, β) to be a worthless edge.

4.2.2 The GreedyChase Algorithm

Algorithm 7. The *GreedyChase* Algorithm

Input: An operator tree
Output: A monotone operator tree
1. **while** there exists some worthless edge (i, j)
2.   Collapse(i,j)
3. **end while**

Since each collapse reduces the number of nodes, *GreedyChase* must terminate. The check for the existence of a worthless edge is the crucial determinant of the running time. When a worthless edge is collapsed, adjacent edges may turn worthless and thus need to be rechecked. The algorithm may be implemented to run in time $O(nd)$, where n is the number of nodes and d is the maximum degree of any node. Experimentally, the running time of our implementation of *GreedyChase* was virtually linear in n.

We remark that even though the order in which new edges turn worthless may depend on the order of edge collapses, the monotone tree for an operator tree is unique.

4.2.3 Lower Bounds

We will use *GreedyChase* as a pre-processing step in all our algorithms. The following lower bounds will be useful in analyzing the performance ratios of our algorithms.

Lemma 4.2.1. *Let $R_i = [t_i + \sum_{j \in V} c_{ij}]$ be the net weight of node i. The response time of any schedule (independent of number of processors) for a monotone operator tree has a lower bound of $R = \max_{i \in V} R_i$.*

Proof. It suffices to show $t_i + \sum_{j \in V} c_{ij}$ to be a lower bound for any node i. Suppose Y is the set of all nodes that are assigned the same processor as i. Y may be decomposed into maximal connected sets $Y_1, \ldots, Y_q$. Suppose $i \in Y_\alpha$. Since $cost(Y) = \sum_j cost(Y_j)$, we have $cost(Y) \geq cost(Y_\alpha)$. By definition of monotone trees, $cost(Y_\alpha) \geq cost(\{i\})$. Thus, the load on the processor executing i is at least $cost(\{i\})$ which is $t_i + \sum_{j \in V} c_{ij}$.

Lemma 4.2.2. *The response time of a p processor schedule for any operator tree (monotone or not) has a lower bound of $\overline{W} = W/p$ where $W = \sum_i t_i$ is the total node weight.*

Proof. The total load is at least the sum of the node weights and some processor must have at least the average load.

4.3 The Modified LPT Algorithm

The *modified LPT* algorithm consists of running *GreedyChase* followed by *LPT*.

Example 4.3.1. Figure 4.2(A) shows traces the collapse of worthless edges by *GreedyChase*. Note that edges may turn worthless as a result of other collapses. For two processors, *modified LPT* produces schedule (B) with response time 11. *Naive LPT* on the other hand may produce schedule (C) with response time 25.

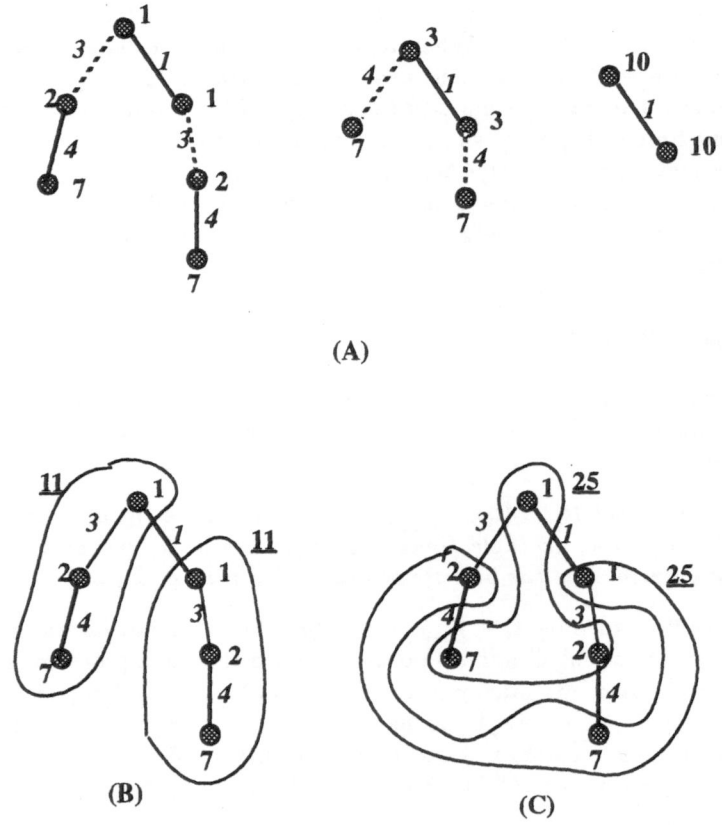

(A)

(B)   (C)

Fig. 4.2. (A) Trace of *GreedyChase* (Worthless Edges Hatched) (B) Modified LPT Schedule (C) Naive LPT Schedule

Modified LPT performs well when the *LPT* stage receives a monotone tree that is star-shaped. Edges in a star have low communication costs since the weight of an edge cannot exceed the weight of the incident leaf without making the edge worthless.

Theorem 4.3.1. *For trees that result in monotone stars, the worst-case performance ratio of the* modified LPT *algorithm is less than* $2 + \frac{1}{p}$. *Examples exist that achieve a ratio of 2.*

Proof. Consider a star in which the center node, labeled 0, is connected to $n-1$ nodes labeled $1, \ldots, n-1$. Let c_i be the weight of the edge from node 0 to node i. If all edges are cut, we get n jobs. The job created from the center has weight $\alpha_0 = t_0 + \sum_{1 \leq i < n} c_i$ and the remaining $n-1$ jobs have weights $\alpha_i = t_i + c_i$ for $i = 1, \ldots, n-1$.

Suppose *LPT* schedules these jobs to give a response time of L. Let j be the node that when scheduled caused the load on some processor to reach L. Since *LPT* assigns a job to the least loaded processor, the load on all processors must have been at least $L - \alpha_j$ when j was assigned. Thus the total load on all processors has to be at least $(L - \alpha_j)p + \alpha_j$.

$$(L - \alpha_j)p + \alpha_j \;\leq\; \sum_{0 \leq i < n} \alpha_i$$

$$L \;\leq\; (1 - \frac{1}{p})\alpha_j + \frac{1}{p}\sum_{0 \leq i < n} \alpha_i$$

$$= (1 - \frac{1}{p})\alpha_j + \frac{1}{p}[\sum_{0 \leq i < n} t_i + 2\sum_{0 \leq i < n} c_i]$$

The above steps are analogous to a standard analysis of the *LPT* algorithm. We can now exploit a property particular to stars. Since all edges are incident with node 0, $\sum_{1 \leq i < n} c_i < \alpha_0$.

$$L \;<\; (1 - \frac{1}{p})\alpha_j + (\sum_{0 \leq i < n} t_i)/p + \frac{2}{p}\alpha_0$$

Since the star is monotone, by Lemmas 4.2.1 and 4.2.2, both α_j and $(\sum t_i)/p$ are lower bounds on the optimal response time L_{opt}. Thus we conclude $L/L_{opt} < 2 + \frac{1}{p}$.

A ratio of 2 is achieved by a star consisting of (p+1) nodes. The center with weight 1 is connected by edges with weight 0 to (p-1) nodes with weight 2, and by an edge of weight $1 - \epsilon$ to a node of weight 1. The optimal schedule achieves a response time of 2 by placing the two nodes of weight 1 on the same processor and the remaining $p-1$ nodes on distinct processors. The *LPT* stage of *Modified LPT* gets $(p-1)$ nodes of weight 2 and 2 nodes of weight $2 - \epsilon$. It therefore produces a schedule with response time $4 - 2\epsilon$.

The algorithm is still oblivious to the tradeoff between parallelism and communication. Edges in a monotone path can have high weights. The algorithm does not attempt to save heavy edges by assigning the incident nodes to the same processor.

Lemma 4.3.1. *The worst-case performance ratio of* modified LPT *is unbounded for paths.*

Proof. Figure 4.3 shows a monotone path for which the *LPT* phase receives n jobs each of weight $2 + \epsilon$. It can produce a schedule with a response time of $(2 + \epsilon)n/p \approx 2n/p$. The optimal is obtained by cutting the path into p pieces of equal length thus obtaining a response time of $2 + \lceil n/p \rceil \epsilon \approx 2$ and a performance ratio of n/p.

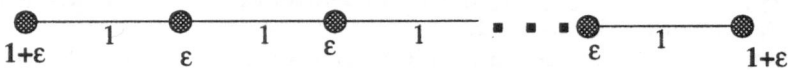

Fig. 4.3. Example with Performance Ratio $= n/p$ for *Modified LPT*

4.4 Connected Schedules

A *connected* schedule requires the nodes assigned to any processor to be a connected set. This restriction is equivalent to only considering schedules that incur communication cost on $p-1$ edges (the minimal possible number) when using p processors.

A practical reason for investigating connected schedules is execution efficiency. Code generation schemes such as that employed in the LDL system [CGK90] generate a *single* thread of control for a connected sets of operators. The context switching between operators is efficiently built into the generated code rather than being managed by more expensive mechanisms such as thread packages. Unconnected sets require as many threads as the number of connected components in the set. Thus connected schedules permit a faster implementation of intra-processor context switching.

While POT is NP-hard, we show that the optimal connected schedule can be constructed by a polynomial algorithm. Subsequent sections show the optimal connected schedule to also be a near-optimal general schedule for path-shaped trees. It therefore finds a use in the construction of the *Hybrid* algorithm in Section 4.6.

A connected schedule for p processors divides the operator tree into $k \leq p$ *fragments* (i.e. connected components) obtained by cutting $k - 1$ edges and collapsing the remaining edges (Figure 4.4). Thus, one way of finding a connected schedule is to examine all $O(2^n)$ combinations of cutting/collapsing edges. The next section shows how we can do better.

4.4.1 Connected Schedules When Communication is Free

We now develop an algorithm for finding the optimal connected schedule for trees in which all edge weights are zero. The algorithm is generalized to handle edge weights in the next section.

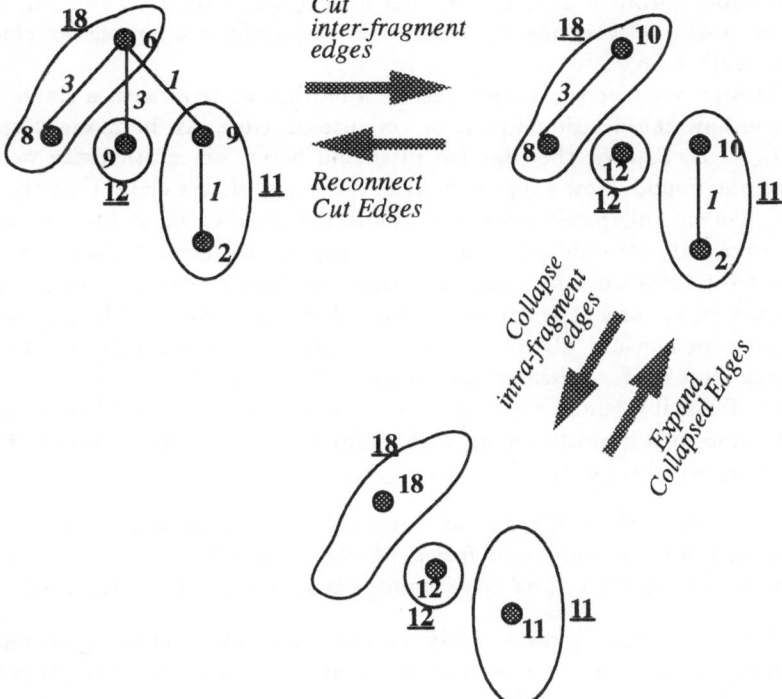

Fig. 4.4. Connected Schedule as Cutting and Collapsing Edges

We will develop the algorithm in two steps. First, given a bound B and number of processors p, we develop an efficient way of finding a connected schedule with a response time of at most B, if such a schedule exists. Second, we show that starting with B set to a lower bound on the response time, we can use a small number of upward revisions to get to the optimal connected schedule.

Definition 4.4.1. *A schedule is (B, p)-bounded if and only if it is a connected schedule that uses at most p processors and has a response time of at most B.*

Definition 4.4.2. *A node is a* mother node *if and only if all adjacent nodes with at most one exception are leaves. The leaf nodes are termed the children of the mother node.*

We first consider the simple case of a mother node m with a single child r to see how the decision to cut or collapse an edge can be made. Suppose $t_r + t_m > B$. Clearly, the edge (m, r) should be cut since otherwise we shall exceed the bound. Now suppose instead $t_r + t_m \leq B$. We claim that the edge (m, r) can be collapsed. Since r is connected only to m, if the connecting edge were cut, r would get a processor, say p_r, to itself. Putting m on p_r reduces the total work for other processors without causing the bound to be exceeded on p_r, and thus can never hurt. This basic idea will be generalized to derive an efficient algorithm. Some of the ideas are similar to those of Hadlock [Had74] for a related but different problem.

The following lemmas narrow the set of schedules we need to examine. We assume m is a mother node with children $r_1, \ldots, r_d$ in the order of non-decreasing weight, i.e. $t_{r_1} \leq t_{r_2} \leq \ldots \leq t_{r_d}$.

Lemma 4.4.1. *If a (B, p)-bounded schedule S places m and r_j in the same fragment and r_i in a different fragment where $i < j$ (i.e. $t_{r_i} \leq t_{r_j}$), then the schedule S' in which r_j and r_i exchange places is also (B, p)-bounded.*

Proof. Let F_m and F_l respectively be the fragments containing m and r_i. Swapping r_i and r_j cannot increase the cost of F_m since $t_{r_i} \leq t_{r_j}$. It suffices to show that the cost of F_l does not increase beyond B. Since S is a connected schedule and leaf r_i is not in the same fragment as its mother node, r_i must be the *only* node in F_l. Since the original schedule was (B, p)-bounded, no individual node weight exceeds B. Thus swapping cannot increase the cost of F_l beyond B.

Repeated application of Lemma 4.4.1 results in:

Lemma 4.4.2. *If there exists a (B, p)-bounded schedule, then there exists a (B, p)-bounded schedule such that (1) if (m, r_j) is collapsed then so is (m, r_{j-1}) (2) if (m, r_j) is cut then so is (m, r_{j+1})*

Let l be the largest number of children that can be collapsed with m without exceeding bound B, that is, the maximum l such that $t_m + \sum_{1 \le i \le l} t_{r_i} \le B$

Theorem 4.4.1. *If there exists a (B, p)-bounded schedule, then there exists a (B, p)-bounded schedule such that (1) (m, r_j) is collapsed for $1 \le j \le l$ (2) (m, r_j) is cut for $l < j \le d$.*

Proof. By Lemma 4.4.2 there exists a (B, p) schedule such that all collapsed children precede all cut children. Assume $t_{r_1}, \ldots t_{r_{l'}}$ are collapsed and $t_{r_{l'+1}}, \ldots, t_d$ are cut. Let F be the fragment containing $m, t_{r_1}, \ldots t_{r_{l'}}$.

Clearly $l' \le l$ since otherwise the bound B will be exceeded. Since $cost(F) \le B$, we can replace the fragments $F, \{t_{r_{l'+1}}\}, \ldots, \{t_{r_l}\}$ by two fragments $F - \{m, t_{r_1}, \ldots, t_{r_{l'}}\}$ and $\{m, t_{r_1}, \ldots t_{r_l}\}$ each of which is bounded.

Theorem 4.4.1 gives us a way of finding a (B, p)-bounded schedule or showing that no such schedule exists. We pick a mother node and traverse the children in the order of non-increasing weights. We collapse children into the mother node as long the weight of the mother stays below B and then cut off the rest. We repeat the process until no more mother nodes are left or we have cut $p - 1$ edges. If the weight of the last fragment is no more than B, we have found a (B, p)-bounded schedule, otherwise no such schedule is possible.

Algorithm 8. The *BpSchedule* Algorithm

Input: Operator tree T with zero edge wts, bound B
Output: Partition of T into fragments $F_1, \ldots, F_p$
        s.t. $cost(F_i) \le B$ for $i = 1, \ldots, p - 1$
1. **while** there exists a mother node m
2.   Let m have children $r_1, \ldots, r_d$ s.t. $t_{r_1} \le \ldots \le t_{r_d}$
3.   Let $l \le d$ be the max l s.t. $t_m + \sum_{1 \le i \le l} t_{r_i} \le B$
4.   **for** $j = 1$ **to** l **do**
5.   collapse(m, r_j)
6.   **for** $j = l + 1$ **to** d **do**
7.   cut(m, r_j)
8.   **if** total number of cuts is $p - 1$ **goto** 10
9. **end while**
10. **return** resulting fragments $F_1, \ldots, F_p$

We will find the optimal connected schedule by setting B to a lower bound on the response time and repeatedly revising B by as large an increment as possible while ensuring that we do not overshoot the optimal value. For each such value of B we run *BpSchedule* and check whether $cost(F_p)$ is at most B.

We can use an unsuccessful run of *BpSchedule* to derive an improved lower bound. For each fragment F_i produced by *BpSchedule*, let B_i be the cost of the fragment plus the weight of the *next* node that was not included in the fragment (i.e. the value t_{l+1} when a cut is made in line 7 of *BpSchedule*). For a re-run to be successful, some fragment must become larger. Thus B must increase to at least B^*, the smallest of the B_i.

Lemma 4.4.3. $B^* = \min_i B_i$ *is a lower bound on the optimal response time.*

Using the lower bounds given by Lemmas 4.2.1 and 4.2.2 and the revision procedure given by Lemma 4.4.3, we devise the algorithm shown below.

Algorithm 9. The *BalancedCuts* Algorithm
Input: Operator tree T with zero edge weights, number of processors p
Output: Optimal connected schedule
1. $B = \max\left(\lceil \sum_{i \in V} t_i / p \rceil, \max_{i \in V} t_i\right)$
2. **repeat forever**
3. $F_1, \ldots, F_p = \text{BpSchedule}(T, B)$
4.   **if** $cost(F_p) \leq B$ **return** $F_1, \ldots, F_p$
5.   Let $B_i = cost(F_i) +$ wt of next node not in F_i
6. $B = \min_i B_i$
7. **end repeat**

The following theorem shows *BalancedCuts* to terminate in at most $O(np)$ iterations and thus have a running time of $O(n^2 p)$. The remarks below show how the implementation may be improved to $O(np)$.

Lemma 4.4.4. BalancedCuts *terminates in at most* $1 + (p-1)(n-p)$ *iterations.*

Proof. Suppose we label the edges by integers starting at 1 in the order they were considered by *BpSchedule*. Any schedule can now be described by a vector $c = c_1, \ldots, c_{p-1}$ of the indices of the $p-1$ cut edges. Notice that $c_1 < c_2 < \ldots < c_{p-1}$. Given two sequences c and c', we say c is dominated by c' if *every* entry of c is no larger than the corresponding entry of c'. The method for revising B guarantees that the increment is large enough for at least one fragment to increase in size. Thus at least one cut must move to a strictly higher label and no cut moves to an edge with a lower label. The sequence of schedules constructed by *BalancedCuts* gives a sequence of vectors where each vector *strictly* dominates all the preceding vectors. The length of any sequence of such vectors can be at most $1 + (p-1)(n-p)$ since the i'th element of the vector may only change from a minimum value to i to a maximum value of $n - p + i$.

A more careful analysis (and implementation) of this idea gives us a bound of $O(nk)$. Whenever the B value is updated, the total work done in finding a new candidate solution can be charged to the nodes which migrate from a component to a previous one. It is easy to verify that the implementation cost works out to be $O(1)$ for each such node migration. Since any one node can migrate at most p times, the total work can be bounded by $O(np)$.

4.4.2 BalancedCuts with Communication Costs

Generalizing *BalancedCuts* to take care of communication requires two changes. Firstly, the input tree must be pre-processed by running *Greedy-Chase*. Secondly, *BpSchedule* must consider the children of a mother node in the order of non-decreasing $t_i - c_{im}$. Both changes are required to make *BpSchedule* work correctly.

BpSchedule assumes that adding more nodes to a fragment, while retaining connectivity, can only increase its cost. The monotone trees produced by *GreedyChase* guarantee exactly this property. Since the schedule for the original tree can be recovered from the schedule for the "pre-processed" tree, it suffices to schedule the monotone tree.

BpSchedule greedily "grows" fragments by collapsing children with their mother node as long as the fragment cost remains bounded. The children were ordered by non-decreasing weights, and the weight of each child was a measure of how much the weight of the fragment would increase by collapsing the child into the mother node. With non-zero edge weights, the mother node must pay the cost of communicating with the child when it is a different fragment. Thus collapsing the child i with the mother m increases the cost of the fragment by $t_i - c_{im}$. Ordering the children of the mother node in the order of non-decreasing $t_i - c_{im}$ suffices to generalize Lemmas 4.4.1 and 4.4.2 and Theorem 4.4.1.

4.5 Connected Schedules as an Approximation

The optimal connected schedule is a good approximation for paths but not for stars.

Theorem 4.5.1. *For path-shaped operator trees, the worst-case performance ratio in using the optimal connected schedule is at most $2 - 1/p$. Examples exist that achieve a ratio of $2 - \frac{1}{\lceil \frac{p+1}{2} \rceil}$.*

Proof. We shall prove the theorem by considering the situation preceding the last iteration of the *BalancedCuts* algorithm (Algorithm 9).

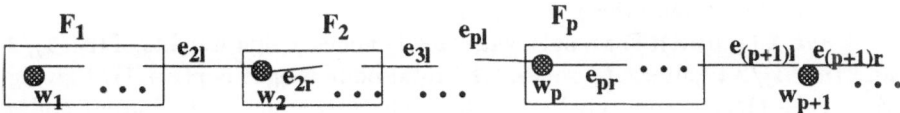

Fig. 4.5. Fragments Formed by *BpSchedule* Before the Last Stage of *BalancedCuts*

Suppose the *BpSchedule* procedure chooses mother nodes in a left-to-right manner, thereby cutting the path into maximal fragments $F_1, \ldots, F_p$

(see Figure 4.5). Let the first node of fragment F_i have weight w_i, and let the weights of the edges to the left and right of w_i be e_{il} and e_{ir}, respectively (take $e_{1l} = 0$, and if w_{p+1} is the last node, take $e_{(p+1)r} = 0$). Let $A_i = cost(F_i)$ and $B_i = cost(F_i \cup \{w_{i+1}\})$.

The procedure for revising bounds chooses the minimum of the B_i's. Therefore before the last round we must have, for $i = 1, \ldots, p$, that $B_i \geq L_C$ where L_C is the response time of the connected schedule. Adding these p inequalities, and using $B_i = cost(F_i \cup \{w_{i+1}\}) = A_i + w_{i+1} + e_{(i+1)r} - e_{(i+1)l}$ we get the following inequality.

$$\sum_{1 \leq i \leq p} (A_i + w_{i+1} + e_{(i+1)r} - e_{(i+1)l}) \geq pL_C$$

This may be rearranged as follows (recall that $e_{1l} = 0$).

$$\frac{1}{p} \left[w_{p+1} + e_{(p+1)r} + \sum_{1 \leq i \leq p} (A_i - e_{il} - e_{(i+1)l}) \right] +$$

$$\frac{1}{p} \left[\sum_{1 < i \leq p} (w_i + e_{il} + e_{ir}) \right] \geq L_C$$

Note that $(A_i - e_{il} - e_{(i+1)l})$ is the sum of the all node weights in the i'th fragment. Further, since there are no worthless edges, $e_{(p+1)r}$ is less than the sum of the weights of all nodes to the right of w_{p+1}. Therefore, $[w_{p+1} + e_{(p+1)r} + \sum_{1 \leq i \leq p}(A_i - e_{il} - e_{(i+1)l})]$ is at most the sum of all node weights. Further, $(w_i + e_{il} + e_{ir})$ is the weight of a node plus the weight of incident edges. Letting $\overline{W}$ (sum of nodes weights divided by p) and R (maximum node weight plus incident edges) represent the lower bounds given by Lemmas 4.2.1 and 4.2.2, the last equation may be rewritten as $\overline{W} + \frac{p-1}{p} R \geq L_C$.

Letting L_{opt} be the response time of the optimal unconnected schedule, $L_{opt} + \frac{p-1}{p} L_{opt} \geq L_C$, or equivalently $\frac{L_C}{L_{opt}} \leq 2 - \frac{1}{p}$.

We now demonstrate examples that achieve a ratio of $2 - 1/\lceil \frac{p+1}{2} \rceil$ i.e., $2p/(p+1)$ for odd values of p and $(2p+2)/(p+2)$ for even values. We will construct examples for which $L_C/\overline{W}$ equals the claimed ratio. We then show that when n is large enough, L_{opt} equals $\overline{W}$ (see Figure 4.6). We will consider the cases of odd and even p separately.

Case 1 (p odd): For a path with $(p+1)$ nodes assign weights of $(p-1)/2$ and $(p+1)/2$ to alternate nodes. The total node weight is $p(p+1)/2$ giving $\overline{W} = (p+1)/2$. A connected schedule needs to combine two adjacent nodes and will therefore have a response time of p giving $L_C/\overline{W} = 2p/(p+1)$.

We now show paths with $p + d$ nodes for which $L_C/L_{opt} = L_C/\overline{W} = 2p/(p+1)$ when $d \geq (p+1)/2$. Such paths are constructed by replacing an end-node (with weight $(p-1)/2$) by d nodes with the same *total* weight. Thus L_C and $\overline{W}$ remain constant but it becomes possible for an unconnected

p	n	EXAMPLE
2	3	$L_C/L_{opt} = 3/2$ $L_C/W = 3/2$ 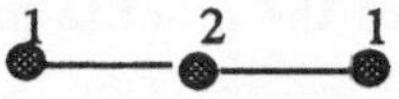
	4	$L_C/L_{opt} = 3/2$ $L_C/W = 3/2$ 
3	4	$L_C/L_{opt} = 3/2$ $L_C/W = 3/2$
	5	$L_C/L_{opt} = 3/2$ $L_C/W = 3/2$ 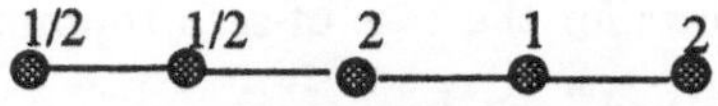
4	5	$L_C/L_{opt} = 5/4$ $L_C/W = 5/3$ 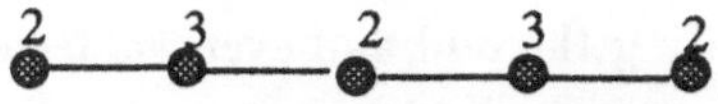
	6	$L_C/L_{opt} = 5/3$ $L_C/W = 5/3$ 
5	6	$L_C/L_{opt} = 5/4$ $L_C/W = 5/3$ 
	7	$L_C/L_{opt} = 5/3$ $L_C/W = 5/3$ 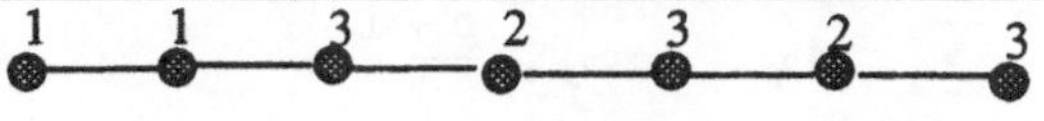

Fig. 4.6. Examples with $\frac{L_C}{L_{opt}} = 2 - \frac{1}{\lceil \frac{p+1}{2} \rceil}$

schedule to obtain a response time of $\overline{W}$ by appropriately matching the new nodes with the lighter nodes. The weight $(p-1)/2$ may be distributed among the d new nodes as follows: give weight 1 to the first $(p-3)/2$ nodes and equally distribute the remaining weight of 1 among the remaining nodes. Now, an unconnected schedule may pair each of the nodes of weight 1 with a node with weight $(p-1)/2$ and put all nodes with weight less than 1 with the remaining node of weight $(p-1)/2$.

Case 2 (p even): For a path with $(p+1)$ nodes assign weights $p/2$ and $1+p/2$ to alternate nodes. We obtain $\overline{W} = (p+2)/2$ and $L_C = p+1$ thus giving $L_C/\overline{W} = (2p+2)/(p+2)$. The remaining argument is similar to Case 1.

There is a small gap between proved worst-case performance ratio of $2-1/p$ and the examples that achieve $2 - 1/\lceil\frac{p+1}{2}\rceil$. The following theorem tightens the proof to meet the examples for the case of zero communication costs.

Theorem 4.5.2. *For path-shaped operator trees with zero communication costs the worst-case performance ratio in using the optimal connected schedule is* $2 - \frac{1}{\lceil\frac{p+1}{2}\rceil}$.

Proof. From the proof of last lemma, the condition $B_i \geq L_C$ may be written as follows for the case of zero communication costs:

$$A_i + w_{i+1} \geq L_C \qquad\qquad \text{for } i = 1,\ldots,p \qquad\qquad (4.4)$$

Separating the odd and even values of p, it suffices to show

$$\frac{L_C}{L_{opt}} \leq \begin{array}{l} \frac{2p}{p+1} \quad \text{for } p \text{ odd} \\ \frac{2p+2}{p+2} \quad \text{for } p \text{ even} \end{array} \qquad\qquad (4.5)$$

Case 1 (p odd): Adding up the $\frac{p+1}{2}$ equations for the odd values of i in (4.4), we have

$$\sum_{1\leq j\leq \frac{p+1}{2}} A_{2j-1} + w_{2j} \geq \frac{p+1}{2}L_C \qquad\qquad (4.6)$$

Observing $A_{2j} \geq w_{2j}$,

$$w_{p+1} + \sum_{1\leq i\leq p} A_i \geq \frac{p+1}{2}L_C \qquad\qquad (4.7)$$

The lhs is at most W, the sum of all node weights. Since W/p is a lower bound, $pL_{opt} \geq W$. Thus we have

$$pL_{opt} \geq \frac{p+1}{2}L_C$$
$$\equiv \quad \frac{L_C}{L_{opt}} \leq \frac{2p}{p+1}$$

Case 2 (p even): Adding up the $\frac{p}{2}$ equations for the odd values of i and the equation for $i = p$ in (4.4), we have

$$A_p + w_{p+1} + \sum_{1 \le j \le \frac{p}{2}} A_{2j-1} + w_{2j} \ge \frac{p+2}{2} L_C$$

Using $A_{2j} \ge w_{2j}$ and rearranging,

$$w_{p+1} + (w_p + \sum_{1 \le i \le p} A_i) \ge \frac{p+2}{2} L_C$$

Note that $w_p + \sum_{1 \le i \le p} A_i$ is at most W and $pL_{opt} \ge W$. Further $L_{opt} \ge w_{p+1}$ since the weight of any node is a lower bound (Lemma 4.2.2). Therefore,

$$L_{opt} + pL_{opt} \ge \frac{p+2}{2} L_C$$
$$\equiv \quad \frac{L_C}{L_{opt}} \le \frac{2p+2}{p+2}$$

Connected schedules are not a good approximation for stars since all fragments except the one containing the center are forced to consist of a single node.

Lemma 4.5.1. *The worst-case performance ratio in using the optimal connected schedule is unbounded for stars.*

Proof. Consider a star in which all nodes have weight 1 and all edges have weight zero. A connected schedule is forced to place a single leaf on all processors except one, and the remaining star on the remaining processor. Thus a connected schedule has a response time of $n - p + 1$. An unconnected schedule achieves a response time of $\lceil n/p \rceil$. Thus, the performance ratio is $(n - p + 1)/\lceil n/p \rceil$ which may have an arbitrarily high value. Figure 4.7 shows an example for $n = 10$ and $p = 5$ that achieves a performance ratio of 3.

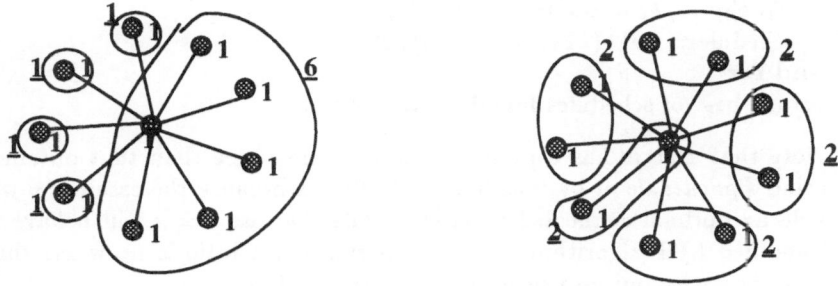

Fig. 4.7. Performance Ratio=3 for Star of 10 Nodes Scheduled on 5 Processors

4.6 Heuristics for POT Scheduling

We now describe two heuristics for the POT problem. We show the heuristics to have worst-case performance ratios of about 2 for several restricted cases. We failed to generate counter-examples even by use of simulations over millions of examples and therefore conjecture these heuristics to have a worst-case performance ratio of about 2 in general.

We have the interesting situation in which the *modified LPT* algorithm works well for stars but not for paths, while connected schedules are a good approximation for paths but not for stars. This naturally motivates the combination of the two algorithms into a *Hybrid* algorithm (Section 4.6.1). In Section 4.6.2, we discuss the *GreedyPairing* algorithm which has the advantage of being extremely simple.

4.6.1 A Hybrid Algorithm

BalancedCuts performs poorly on stars since the constraint of connected schedules is at odds with load balancing. While the algorithm is cognizant of communication costs, it is poor at achieving balanced loads. On the other hand, *LPT* is very good at balancing loads but unaware of communication costs.

One way of combining the two algorithms is to use *BalancedCuts* to cut the tree into many fragments and then schedule the fragments using *LPT*. *LPT* can be expected to "cleanup" cases such as stars on which connected schedules are a bad approximation.

Algorithm 10. The *Hybrid* Algorithm

Input: Operator tree T, number of processors p
Output: A schedule
1.   T' = GreedyChase(T)
 2. **for** i = p **to** n **do**
3. $F_1, F_2, \ldots, F_i = BalancedCuts(T', i)$
 4.   schedule = $LPT(\{F_1, F_2, \ldots, F_i\}, p)$
5.   **end for**
6.   return best of schedules found in steps 2 to 5

Note that *Hybrid* has a performance ratio no worse than that obtained by using *BpSchedule* or by *modified LPT*. This is because the case $i = p$ will provide an optimal connected schedule, while the case $i = n$ will behave as the modified LPT algorithm. Thus the performance ratio is no worse than $2 - 1/p$ for paths and no worse than $2 + 1/p$ for stars.

4.6.2 The Greedy Pairing Algorithm

We now describe an algorithm which is based on greedily collapsing that pair of nodes which leads to the least increase in response time.

GreedyPairing starts by first pre-processing the operator tree into a monotone tree by running *GreedyChase*. Then it chooses the pair of nodes, i and j, such that $cost(\{i, j\})$ is the minimum possible and collapses them. Ties are broken by favoring the pair which offers the greatest reduction in communication. This process is continued until the number of nodes is reduced to p, and then each node is assigned a distinct processor. Note that collapsing two (non-adjacent) nodes in a tree will not necessarily maintain the property of being a tree.

We can prove the algorithm to have a worst-case performance ratio close to 2 for the case of zero edge weights.

Theorem 4.6.1. *The* GreedyPairing *algorithm has a tight worst-case performance ratio of* $2 - 2/(p+1)$ *when all edge weights are zero.*

Proof. Consider the penultimate stage of this algorithm, i.e. when there remain $p + 1$ nodes. Label the nodes as $0, 1, \ldots, p$. Without loss of generality, assume that the last collapse is of the pair $S = \{0, 1\}$.

We first claim that if the response time L of the final schedule is not given by $cost(S) = t_0 + t_1$ then *GreedyPairing* produces an optimal schedule. Suppose that the response time is larger than $cost(S)$, then there exists an $i > 1$ such that $t_i > t_0 + t_1$. But then i must be one of the original nodes, since *GreedyPairing* would always prefer to collapse the nodes 0 and 1 before ever performing the collapse which would result in a node of cost t_i. Since t_i is a lower bound (Lemma 4.2.1) on the optimal response time, we obtain that the response time $L = t_i$ is optimal.

Consider now the remaining case where $L = cost(S) = t_0 + t_1$. By the definition of *GreedyPairing*, we have that for all $i, j \in \{0, 1, \ldots, p\}$, $L = t_0 + t_1 \leq t_i + t_j$. Summing over all i and j, we obtain that

$$\frac{p(p+1)}{2} L \leq \sum_{0 \leq i < j \leq p} (t_i + t_j)$$
$$= p \sum_{i=0}^{p} t_i$$
$$\leq p^2 L_{opt}$$

where the last inequality follows from Lemmas 4.2.2 and 4.2.1. We conclude that $L \leq \frac{2p}{p+1} L_{opt}$ which gives the desired bound on the performance ratio.

That this bound is tight can be seen from the following example. Suppose there are p nodes of weight 1 and p nodes of weight p. The optimal solution pairs off one node of each type achieving a response time of $p + 1$. On the other hand, *GreedyPairing* merges the nodes of weight 1 to obtain, at the penultimate stage, $p + 1$ nodes of weight p. At this point it is forced to pair two nodes of weight p each, giving a response time of $2p$.

4.7 Approximation Algorithms

We first discuss a two-stage approach to developing approximation algorithms and then develop the *LocalCuts* and *BoundedCuts* algorithms.

4.7.1 A Two-Stage Approach

We divide the POT scheduling problem into two stages, *fragmentation* followed by *scheduling*. Fragmentation produces a connected schedule assuming unlimited processors. Scheduling assigns the fragments produced by the first stage to the real processors.

The two stage approach offers conceptual simplicity and does not restrict the space of schedules. Any schedule defines a natural fragmentation corresponding to cutting exactly the inter-processor edges. For any given schedule, some scheduling algorithm will produce it from its natural fragmentation. Notice that the scheduling stage may assign two fragments that were connected by a cut edge to the same processor thus "undoing" the cutting. Thus, several fragmentations may produce the same schedule. In our analysis, we will ignore the decrease in communication cost caused by this implicit undoing of an edge cutting operation. This can only over-estimate the cost of our solution.

The two-stage approach allows us to use standard multiprocessor scheduling algorithms for the second stage. We choose to use the LPT [Gra69] algorithm. Given the use of LPT for scheduling, we may develop the conditions for a good fragmentation. There is an inherent tradeoff between total load and the weight of the heaviest connected fragment. If an edge is cut, communication cost is incurred thus increasing total load. If an edge is collapsed, a new node with a larger net weight is created, potentially increasing the weight of the largest connected fragment. Lemma 4.7.3 captures this trade-off and provides conditions on fragmentation for a bounded performance ratio.

Recall our choice of notation from Section 4.2.3. $R_i = t_i + \sum_j c_{ij}$ is the net weight of node i and $R = \max_i R_i$. $W = \sum_i t_i$ is the sum of the weights of all nodes and $\overline{W} = W/p$ is the average node weight per processor.

Assuming fragmentation to produces q fragments with weights $M_1, \ldots, M_q$, we make the following definitions.

Definition 4.7.1. $M = \max_i M_i$ *is the weight of heaviest fragment. C is the the total communication cost incurred, which is twice the sum of the weights of the cut edges. $\overline{L} = (W + C)/p$ is the average load per processor.*

We use the subscript OPT to denote the same quantities for the natural fragmentation corresponding to an optimal schedule, for example, M_{opt} for the weight of the heaviest fragment. We have:

Lemma 4.7.1. $\overline{W} \leq \overline{L} \leq L$. *In particular, $\overline{W} \leq \overline{L}_{opt} \leq L_{opt}$.*

Lemma 4.7.2. $R \leq M \leq L$. *In particular, $R \leq M_{opt} \leq L_{opt}$.*

In the following lemma, k_1 captures the effect of size of the largest fragment and k_2 the load increase due to communication.

Lemma 4.7.3. *Given a fragmentation with $M \leq k_1 L_{opt}$ and $\overline{L} \leq k_2 \overline{L}_{opt}$, scheduling using LPT yields a schedule with $L/L_{opt} \leq \max\{k_1, 2k_2\}$.*

Proof. Let p_k be a *heaviest* loaded processor in an *LPT* schedule with response time L. Let M_j be the last fragment assigned to p_k. We will divide the analysis into two cases based on whether M_j is the only fragment on p_k or not.

If M_j is the only fragment on p_k, $L = M_j$ and by our assumption,

$$L = M_j \leq M \leq k_1 L_{opt}$$

Now consider the case when the number of fragments on p_k is at least 2. Since *LPT* assigns a job to the least loaded processor, the load on *any* processor must be at least $L - M_j$ when M_j was assigned to p_k. The total load $\sum_k L_k$ may be bounded as

$$\sum_k L_k \geq (L - M_j)p + M_j$$

$$\Rightarrow \quad L \leq \frac{1}{p} \sum_k L_k + \left(1 - \frac{1}{p}\right) M_j$$

$$\Rightarrow \quad L \leq \overline{L} + M_j.$$

Since *LPT* chooses the least loaded processor, the first p jobs are scheduled on distinct processors. Since there was at least one other fragment on p_k before M_j, there are at least $p + 1$ fragments, each of them no lighter than M_j. Thus,

$$\sum_k L_k \geq (p + 1)M_j$$

$$\Rightarrow \quad M_j \leq \frac{1}{p+1} \sum_k L_k < \overline{L}.$$

Combining the two inequalities shown above and using the assumption $\overline{L} \leq k_2 \overline{L}_{opt}$, we obtain

$$\begin{aligned} L &\leq \overline{L} + M_j \\ &\leq 2\overline{L} \\ &\leq 2k_2 \overline{L}_{opt}. \end{aligned}$$

Combining the two cases, we conclude $L/L_{opt} \leq \max\{k_1, 2k_2\}$.

Using the above lemma, the best we can do is to find a fragmentation with $k_1 = k_2 = 1$ which would guaranteed a performance ratio of 2. However, finding the best fragmentation is NP-complete.

Theorem 4.7.1. *Given a star $T = (V, E)$, bounds B and C, the problem of determining whether there is a partition of V such that no fragment is heavier than B and the total communication is no more than C is NP-complete.*

Proof. (Sketch) We reduce the classical *knapsack* problem [GJ79] to the above problem. Let an instance of the knapsack problem be specified by a bag size S and n pairs (w_i, p_i) where each pair corresponds to an object of weight w_i

with profit p_i. We can assume without loss of generality that $p_i \leq w_i$ for all i since all p_i can be scaled. Consider a star T with $n + 1$ nodes obtained from the knapsack instance. We label the nodes of T from 0 to n with the center as 0. We set $c_{i0} = p_i/2$ and $t_i = w_i + c_i$ and $B = S + \sum_i c_i$. We claim that the minimum communication cost for the star instance is C if and only if the maximum profit for the knapsack instance is $\sum_i p_i - C$.

We remark that the problem is polynomially solvable when the tree is restricted to be a path. The next two subsections focus on algorithms to find a fragmentation that guarantees low values for k_1 and k_2.

4.7.2 The LocalCuts Algorithm

We now develop a linear time algorithm for fragmentation called LOCAL-CUTS. We show bounds on the weight of the heaviest fragment as well as on the load increase due to communication. Application of Lemma 4.7.3 shows the algorithm to have a performance ratio of 3.56.

LOCALCUTS repeatedly picks a leaf and determines whether to cut or collapse the edge to its parent. It makes the decision based on *local* information, the ratio of the leaf weight to the weight of the edge to its parent. The basic intuition is that if the ratio is low, then collapsing the edge will not substantially increase the *net* weight of the parent. If the ratio is high, the communication cost incurred by cutting will be relatively low and can be amortized to the weight of the node cut off. One complication is that cutting or collapsing an edge changes node weights. Our analysis *amortizes* the cost of cutting an edge over the total weight of all nodes that were collapsed to produce the leaf.

In the following discussion we assume that the tree T has been *rooted* at some arbitrary vertex. We will refer to the fragment containing the root as the *residual tree*. A *mother* node in a rooted tree is a node all of whose children are leaves. The algorithm uses a parameter $\alpha > 1$. We will later show (Theorem 4.7.2) how this parameter may be chosen to minimize the performance ratio.

Algorithm 11. The *LocalCuts* Algorithm

Input: Monotone operator tree T, parameter $\alpha > 1$.
Output: Partition of T into fragments $F_1, \ldots, F_k$.
1. **while** there is a mother node m with a child j **do**
2.   **if** $t_j > \alpha c_{jm}$ **then** cut e_{jm}
3.   **else** collapse e_{jm}
4. **end while**

The running time of the LOCALCUTS algorithm is $O(n)$. The following lemma shows a bound on the weight of the resulting fragments.

Lemma 4.7.4. *Any fragment produced by* LOCALCUTS *has weight less than* αR, *which implies* $M < \alpha R$.

Proof. Consider an arbitrary fragment produced in the course of the algorithm. Let m be the *highest* level node in the fragment, with children $1, \ldots, d$. The node m is picked as a mother node at some stage of the algorithm. Now, $R_m = c_{mp} + t_m + c_{m1} + \ldots + c_{md}$ where c_{mp} is the weight of the edge from m to it's parent. Collapsing child j into m, corresponds to replacing c_{mj} by t_j. Since the condition for collapsing is $t_j < \alpha c_{mj}$, collapsing children can increase R_m to at most αR_m which is no greater than αR.

We now use an amortization argument to show that the communication cost incurred by the LOCALCUTS algorithm is bounded by a constant factor of the total node weight, W.

Lemma 4.7.5. *The total communication cost of the partition produced by the* LOCALCUTS *algorithm is bounded by* $\frac{2}{\alpha-1}W$, *that is* $C \le \frac{2}{\alpha-1}W$.

Proof. We associate a *credit* p_i with each node i and *credit* p_{jk} with each edge e_{jk}. Initially, edges have zero credit and the credit of a node equals it's weight; thus, the total initial credit is W. The total credit will be conserved as the algorithm proceeds. When a node is cut or collapsed, it's credit is taken away and either transferred to another node or to an edge that is cut. The proof is based on showing that when the algorithm terminates, every edge that is cut has a credit equal to $(\alpha - 1)$ times it's weight. This allows us to conclude that the total weight of the cut edges is bounded by $W/(\alpha - 1)$. This would then imply that $C \le \frac{2}{\alpha-1}W$. We abuse notation by using t_i for the *current* weight of a node in the residual tree. We now prove the following invariants using an inductive argument.

1. Each node has a credit greater than or equal to it's *current* weight in the residual tree, i.e., $p_i \ge t_i$.
2. Each *cut* edge e_{im} has a credit equal to $(\alpha - 1)$ times it's weight, i.e., $p_{im} = (\alpha - 1)c_{im}$.

As the base case, these invariants are trivially true at the beginning of the algorithm. As the inductive step, suppose these invariants are true up to k iterations and we consider leaf node j with mother m in the $(k + 1)$st iteration. If j is collapsed, $t_m^{new} = t_m + t_j$. We use the superscript *new* to indicate the values at the next iteration. By transferring the credit of j to m, we get $p_m^{new} = p_j + p_m$. Since $p_j \ge t_j$ and $p_m \ge t_m$, by the inductive hypothesis we have $p_m^{new} \ge t_m^{new}$ and both invariants are preserved.

If j is cut, $t_m^{new} = t_m + c_{jm}$. We need to transfer a credit of c_{jm} to m to maintain the first invariant. The remaining credit $p_j - c_{jm}$ may be transferred to the edge e_{jm}. By the induction hypothesis, we have $p_j - c_{jm} \ge t_j - c_{jm}$ and since edge e_{jm} was cut, $p_j - c_{jm} > (\alpha - 1)c_{jm}$. Thus sufficient credit is available for the second invariant as well.

The previous two lemmas combined with Lemma 4.7.3, allow us to bound the performance ratio guaranteed by LOCALCUTS. The following theorem states the precise result and provides a value for the parameter α.

Theorem 4.7.2. *Using* LPT *to schedule the fragments produced by* LOCAL-CUTS *with* $\alpha = (3+\sqrt{17})/2$ *gives a performance ratio of* $(3+\sqrt{17})/2 \sim 3.56$.

Proof. From Lemma 4.7.5 and Lemma 4.7.1,

$$\overline{L} = \frac{W+C}{p} \leq \frac{\alpha+1}{\alpha-1}\overline{W} \leq \frac{\alpha+1}{\alpha-1}\overline{L}_{opt}.$$

Combining this with Lemma 4.7.4 and using Lemma 4.7.3 we conclude

$$\frac{L}{L_{opt}} \leq \max\left\{\alpha, \frac{2(\alpha+1)}{\alpha-1}\right\}$$

Observing that the max is minimized when $\alpha = 2(\alpha+1)/(\alpha-1)$, we obtain $\alpha = (3+\sqrt{17})/2$ and $L/L_{opt} \leq (3+\sqrt{17})/2$.

The performance ratio of LOCALCUTS is tight. Consider a star in which the center node with weight δ is connected by edges of weight 1 to $n-1$ leaves, each of weight $\alpha = 3.56$. Suppose the star is scheduled on $p = n$ processors. LOCALCUTS will collapse all leaves and produce a single fragment of weight $(n-1)\alpha + \delta$. The optimal schedule consists of cutting all edges to produce $n-1$ fragments of weight $1+\alpha$ and one fragment of weight $n-1+\delta$. When $n > 5$, the performance ratio is $((n-1)\alpha + \delta)/(n-1+\delta)$ which approaches α as δ goes to zero.

4.7.3 The BoundedCuts Algorithm

The LOCALCUTS algorithm determines whether to collapse a leaf into its mother based on the ratio of the leaf weight to the weight of the edge to its mother. The decision is independent of the current weight of the mother node. From the analysis of LOCALCUTS, we see that the weight of the largest fragment is bounded by αR_m, where m is the highest level node in the fragment (Lemma 4.7.4). If R_m is small compared to M_{opt}, we may cut expensive edges needlessly. Using a bound that is independent of R_m should reduce communication costs.

The analysis of LOCALCUTS showed the trade-off between total communication $(C \leq \frac{2}{\alpha-1}W)$ and the bound on fragment size $(M < \alpha R)$. Reduced communication should allow us to afford a lower value of α, thus reducing the largest fragment size and the performance ratio.

We now discuss a modified algorithm called BOUNDEDCUTS that uses a uniform bound B at each mother node. It also cuts off light edges in a manner similar to LOCALCUTS. Our analysis will show that the modified algorithm improves the performance ratio to 2.87. We will show the ratio to be tight. Our analysis of communication costs uses lower bounds on C_{opt}, the communication incurred in some fixed optimal schedule.

The algorithm below is stated in terms of three parameters α, β and B that are assumed to satisfy $\beta \geq \alpha > 1$, and $M_{opt} \leq B \leq L_{opt}$. Our analysis uses these conditions and we shall later show how the values of these parameters may be fixed.

Algorithm 12. The *BoundedCuts* Algorithm
Input: Monotone operator tree T, real parameters α, β, and B
       where $\beta \geq \alpha > 1$ and $B \geq R$.
Output: Partition of T into connected fragments $T_1, \ldots, T_k$.
1. **while** there exists a mother node m
2.   partition children of m into sets N_1, N_2 such that
        child $j \in N_1$ if and only if $t_j/c_{mj} \geq \beta$;
3.   cut e_{mj} for $j \in N_1$; (β **rule**)
4.   **if** $R_m + \sum_{j \in N_2}(t_j - c_{mj}) \leq \alpha B$ **then**
5.   collapse e_{mj} for all $j \in N_2$
6.   **else** cut e_{mj} for all $j \in N_2$; (α **rule**)
7. **end while**
8. **return** resulting fragments $T_1, \ldots, T_k$.

Lemma 4.7.6. *Any fragment produced by* BOUNDEDCUTS *has weight at most αB. As a consequence, $M \leq \alpha L_{opt}$.*

Proof. Since the weight of a fragment increases only when some edge is collapsed, the explicit check in line 4 ensures the lemma.

Let C denote the set of edges cut by BOUNDEDCUTS. We cut edges using two rules, the β rule in Step 3 and the α rule in Step 6. Let C_β and C_α denote the edges cut using the respective rules. C_β and C_α are disjoint and $C_\beta \cup C_\alpha = C$. Let $\mathcal{C}_\beta$ and $\mathcal{C}_\alpha$ denote the communication cost incurred due to edges in C_β and C_α respectively. We bound $\mathcal{C}_\beta$ and $\mathcal{C}_\alpha$ in Lemmas 4.7.7 and 4.7.9.

Lemma 4.7.7. $\mathcal{C}_\alpha \leq \dfrac{\beta - 1}{\alpha - 1} C_{opt}.$

The proof of the lemma requires several definitions and lemmas.

Definition 4.7.2. *Let $T_i = (V_i, E_i)$ denote a subtree of $T = (V, E)$ rooted at i, defined as follows: V_i includes i, children of i that are not cut off by the β rule, and all nodes that eventually collapse into a child of i; E_i consists of all edges $e_{kj} \in E$ such that $k, j \in V_i$. The weight of an edge in E_i is the same as the corresponding edge in E. The weight of node $j \in V_i$ is the weight of j in T plus the weights of all incident edges that are not in E_i, i.e., $t_j^{(T_i)} = t_j^{(T)} + \sum_{\ell \in V - V_i} c_{j\ell}$.*

Figure 4.8 illustrates the definition of T_i. With respect to the figure, the weight of m in T_m equals the original weight plus the weight of the two edges that connect m to nodes not in T_m.

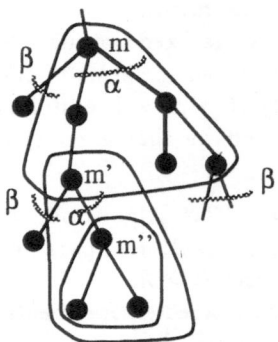

Fig. 4.8. Subtrees T_m, $T_{m'}$, $T_{m''}$ for Nodes m, m', m''

Definition 4.7.3. W_i *is the total weight of all nodes in* T_i.

Definition 4.7.4. C_{opt} *is defined to be the set of edges in tree* T *that are cut in a fixed optimal solution.*

Definition 4.7.5. C_{opt}^i *is set of edges formed by starting with the edges* $C_{opt} \cap E_i$ *and deleting all edges* e_{kj} *for which there exists* $e_{ml} \in C_{opt} \cap E_i$ *with* m *being an ancestor of* k. C_{opt}^i *is a subset of the edges of* T_i *that are cut in the*

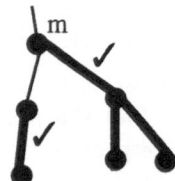

Fig. 4.9. C_{opt}^m

optimal. Figure 4.9 shows the edges in T_m that are cut by a fixed optimal schedule as thick edges. The subset of edges that forms C_{opt}^m are checked off.

Definition 4.7.6. C_α^i *is defined to be the set of edges in tree* T_i *that are cut by the* α *rule.* C_α^i *is the total weight of the edges in* C_α^i.

Lemma 4.7.8. *If* m *and* m' *are distinct mother nodes where we cut using the* α *rule, then* $C_{opt}^m \cap C_{opt}^{m'} = \phi$ *and* $C_\alpha^m \cap C_\alpha^{m'} = \phi$.

Proof. The lemma follows since, by their definition, trees T_m and $T_{m'}$ do not share any edges (see Figure 4.8).

PROOF OF LEMMA 4.7.7

Proof. By Lemma 4.7.8, it suffices to establish

$$C_\alpha^m \le \frac{\beta - 1}{\alpha - 1} C_{opt}^m$$

for each mother node m where we use the α rule to cut edges. Let the set C_{opt}^m consist of s edges $e_{m_1 z_1}, \ldots, e_{m_s z_s}$. These edges partition T_m into $s + 1$ fragments. From the definition of C_{opt}^m it follows that one fragment, F_m, contains nodes m and $m_1, \ldots, m_s$ (some of these may be the same as m). Let the remaining fragments be $F_1, \ldots, F_s$, with F_j containing node z_j. We have

$$C_{opt}^m = \sum_{1 \le j \le s} c_{m_j z_j}$$

Since no fragment in the optimal is larger than M_{opt}, the total node weight in fragment F_m is at most $M_{opt} - \sum_{1 \le j \le s} c_{m_j z_j}$. Thus, letting Q_j be the total node weight in fragment F_j for $j = 1, \ldots, s$, we have

$$M_{opt} - \sum_{1 \le j \le s} c_{m_j z_j} + \sum_{1 \le j \le s} Q_j \ge W_m.$$

We applied the α rule at m. Since children cut by the α rule are in T_m, $W_m > \alpha B$. Since $B \ge M_{opt}$, we have $W_m > \alpha M_{opt}$ which reduces the above equation to:

$$\sum_{1 \le j \le s} (Q_j - c_{m_j z_j}) > (\alpha - 1) M_{opt}$$

Since no edge in T_m was cut by the β rule, we must have $Q_j < \beta c_{m_j z_j}$ which results in

$$\sum_{1 \le j \le s} (\beta - 1) c_{m_j z_j} > (\alpha - 1) M_{opt}$$

$$\Rightarrow \quad M_{opt} < \frac{\beta - 1}{\alpha - 1} \sum_{1 \le j \le s} c_{m_j z_j} = \frac{\beta - 1}{\alpha - 1} C_{opt}^m.$$

Since $C_\alpha^m < R_m \le M_{opt}$, we have the desired result:

$$C_\alpha^m \le \frac{\beta - 1}{\alpha - 1} C_{opt}^m$$

Using techniques similar to those in the proof of Lemma 4.7.5, we show the following bound on C_β.

Lemma 4.7.9. $C_\beta \le \frac{2}{\beta - 1} W - \frac{\alpha - 1}{\beta - 1} C_\alpha.$

Proof. We use a credit based argument similar to that of Lemma 4.7.5. For each edge in C_β we associate a credit of $(\beta - 1)$ times it's weight and for each

C_α edge we maintain a credit of $(\alpha - 1)$ times it's weight. The proof for C_β edges is similar to that in Lemma 4.7.5. For C_α edges, we cannot use a similar argument since the weight of the leaf being cut off, is not necessarily α times the weight of the edge to it's parent. But consider all the edges cut off at a mother node. From the algorithm we have $R_m + \sum_{j \in N_2}(t_j - c_{mj}) > \alpha B$. From this we see that even though each leaf is not heavy enough, the combined weight of all the leaves being cut off at a mother node is sufficient for a credit of $(\alpha - 1)$ times the weight of the edges cut. Since we start with an initial credit of W, the result follows.

Combining Lemmas 4.7.7 and 4.7.9, we obtain the following.

Lemma 4.7.10. $C = C_\beta + C_\alpha \leq \dfrac{2}{\beta - 1}W + \dfrac{\beta - \alpha}{\alpha - 1}C_{opt}.$

We need the following technical lemma before we prove the main theorem.

Lemma 4.7.11. *For $\beta \geq \alpha > 1$, the function*

$$m(\alpha, \beta) = \max\left\{\alpha, \frac{2(\beta + 1)}{\beta - 1}, \frac{2(\beta - \alpha)}{\alpha - 1}\right\}$$

is minimized when

$$\alpha = \frac{2(\beta + 1)}{\beta - 1} = \frac{2(\beta - \alpha)}{\alpha - 1}$$

The minimum value is 2.87 when $\alpha \sim 2.87$ and $\beta \sim 5.57$.

Proof. We observe that $f(\alpha, \beta) = \alpha$ is strictly increasing in α, $h(\alpha, \beta) = 2(\beta - \alpha)/(\alpha - 1)$ is strictly decreasing in α, $g(\alpha, \beta) = 2(\beta + 1)/(\beta - 1)$ is strictly decreasing in β, and h is strictly increasing in β. From this it is easy to verify that at the optimum point, both f and g must be equal to the optimum value. If either them is not the max-value of the max, then appropriately change α/β to make this happen, and note that this can only reduce the value of h. From this it follows that all three terms are equal at the optimum. Eliminating β from the above two equations gives us

$$\alpha^3 - \alpha^2 - 4\alpha - 4 = 0$$

which on solving yields the claimed values for α, β and the minimum.

Theorem 4.7.3. *Using* LPT *to schedule the fragments produced by* BOUND-EDCUTS *with $\alpha = 2.87$, and $\beta = 5.57$ gives a performance ratio of 2.87.*

Proof. Using Lemma 4.7.10, we have

$$\overline{L} = \frac{W + C}{p} \leq W + \frac{2}{\beta - 1}W + \frac{\beta - \alpha}{\alpha - 1}C_{opt}$$

$$\leq \max\left\{\frac{\beta + 1}{\beta - 1}, \frac{\beta - \alpha}{\alpha - 1}\right\} \times \overline{L}_{opt}.$$

Using the bound on $\overline{L}$ from the above equation and from the bound on M from Lemma 4.7.6, we can apply Lemma 4.7.3 to obtain

$$\frac{L}{L_{opt}} \leq \max\left\{\alpha, 2\left(\max\left\{\frac{\beta+1}{\beta-1}, \frac{\beta-\alpha}{\alpha-1}\right\}\right)\right\}$$
$$\leq \max\left\{\alpha, \frac{2(\beta+1)}{\beta-1}, \frac{2(\beta-\alpha)}{\alpha-1}\right\}.$$

From Lemma 4.7.11, the right hand side of the above inequality is minimized at the values stated in the theorem, and this shows that $L/L_{opt} \leq 2.87$.

The performance ratio of BOUNDEDCUTS is tight. The example is similar to that for LOCALCUTS i.e. a star in which the center node with weight δ is connected by edges of weight 1 to $n-1$ leaves each of weight $\alpha = 2.87$. Suppose the star is scheduled on $p = n$ processors. The optimal schedule consists of cutting all edges to produce $n-1$ fragments of weight $1+\alpha$ and one fragment of weight $n-1+\delta$. Taking $n > 4$, $M_{opt} = L_{opt} = n-1+\delta$. BOUNDEDCUTS will collapse all leaves and produce a single fragment of weight $(n-1)\alpha + \delta$ (since $B = L_{opt}$, this does not exceed αB). The performance performance ratio is therefore $((n-1)\alpha + \delta)/(n-1+\delta)$ which approaches α as δ goes to zero.

The results in this section rely on the fact that the bound B used in BOUNDEDCUTS satisfies $M_{opt} \leq B \leq L_{opt}$. Since we do not know the optimal partition, we do not know M_{opt} or L_{opt}. However, we can ensure that we try a value of B that is as close as we want to L_{opt}. The following theorem makes the idea more precise.

Theorem 4.7.4. *For any $\epsilon > 0$, we can ensure that we run BOUNDEDCUTS with a bound B satisfying $L_{opt} \leq B \leq (1+\epsilon)L_{opt}$. This yields a performance ratio of $(1+\epsilon)2.87$ with a running time of $O(\epsilon^{-1}np\log n)$.*

Proof. From Lemmas 4.7.1 and 4.7.2, $\max\{\overline{W}, R\}$ is a lower bound on L_{opt}. W is an upper bound since we can always schedule the entire tree on a single processor. Thus, $\overline{W} \leq L_{opt} \leq p\overline{W}$. We can try the value $B = \epsilon k\overline{W}$ for each integer k satisfying $1/\epsilon \leq k \leq p/\epsilon$. For each such value, we run BOUNDEDCUTS followed by LPT and take the best schedule. This guarantees that we will use a bound $L_{opt} \leq B \leq (1+\epsilon)L_{opt}$. From the previous analysis, if we use such a bound, we get a performance ratio of $(1+\epsilon)2.87$. There are $(p-1)/\epsilon$ values for k, LPT requires $O(n\log n)$ time, and BOUNDEDCUTS requires $O(n)$. Thus the total time for all values of B is $O(\epsilon^{-1}np\log n)$.

4.8 Experimental Comparison

In this section, we experimentally compare the average-case performance of the algorithms developed in previous sections. We first discuss the experimental setup and then describe the results. The overall result is that Hybrid has the best average case behavior.

4.8.1 Experimental Setup

All experiments were done by random sampling from spaces of monotone trees. The space was specified by four parameters: *shape, size, edgeRange* and *nodeRange*. We restricted ourselves to monotone trees since all algorithms pre-process the input tree into a monotone tree.

The shape of trees was controlled by specifying the maximum number of children that a node could have. Given this maximum, the actual number of children of a non-leaf node was randomly chosen from between 1 and the maximum. Two interesting classes of shapes are *narrow* and *wide* trees. Narrow trees restrict a node to have at most two children while wide trees allowed a node to have any number of children. Narrow trees represent the shapes that are commonly encountered in practice since most database operators have 1 or 2 arguments.

EdgeRange and nodeRange specified the integer ranges from which edge and node weights could be chosen. The size specified the number of nodes in the trees to be generated.

Given fixed values for shape, size, edgeRange and nodeRange, we randomly generated trees of at least the given size and filtered those whose corresponding monotone trees was of the exact size needed. For each specification of the space that we experimented with, we generated 2500 monotone trees and stored them in a file.

Each reported data point is an average over 2500 monotone trees. This number of samples was always sufficient to guarantee an error of less than 5% with a confidence of 95%.

4.8.2 Experimental Comparison

All experiments reported in this section are on trees with 30 nodes with both edgeRange and nodeRange set to 1...100. The shapes of the trees are either narrow or wide. We again note that narrow trees represent the shapes that are commonly encountered in practice.

Experiments with spaces in which the tree size or shape was different did not yield any new lessons. Changes to edgeRange and nodeRange do change the difference between curves but did not, in our observation, change the relative ordering of algorithms.

Since computing the optimal schedule has prohibitive cost, all performance ratios are with respect to a lower bound on the optimal. The lower bound was taken to be the largest of two lower bounds. The lower bounds given by Lemma 4.2.2 can be improved using the following lemma. The second lower bound was from Lemma 4.2.1.

Lemma 4.8.1. *If C_E is the sum of the weights of the cheapest $p-1$ edges and W the sum of all node weights in a monotone tree with at least p nodes, then $(C_E + W)/p$ is a lower bound on the optimal response time.*

Proof. The optimal schedule for a monotone tree with at least p nodes must cut at least $p - 1$ edges.

4.8.3 Performance of Hybrid

Figures 4.8.3 and 4.8.3 plot performance ratios for the Hybrid algorithm as well as the two algorithms out of which Hybrid was constructed.

We observe that Modified LPT outperforms BalancedFragments for wide trees but the situation reverses for narrow trees. The explanation lies in the fact that narrow trees are close to paths while wide trees are close to stars. Connected schedules produced by BalancedFragments are a good approximation for paths (Theorem 4.5.1) but not for stars (Lemma 4.5.1). Schedules produced by Modified LPT are a good approximation for stars (Theorem 4.3.1) but not for paths (Lemma 4.3.1).

Hybridization of the two algorithms helps since for an *specific* tree either one or the other algorithm performs well.

Avg. Performance Ratio

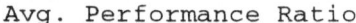
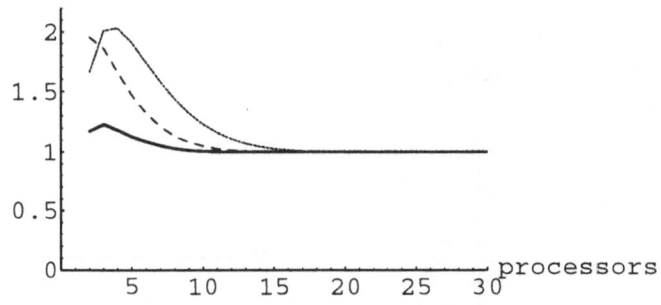

Fig. 4.10. Performance of Hybrid (Solid), BalancedFragments (Dotted) and Modified LPT (Dashed) on Wide Trees

4.8.4 Comparison of Hybrid, LocalCuts and BoundedCuts

Figures 4.8.4 and 4.8.4 compare Hybrid, LocalCuts and BoundedCuts.

We first observe that even though BoundedCuts has a better worst-case performance ratio than LocalCuts, LocalCuts performs better on the average. The explanation lies in the fact that while the weight of the largest fragment is lower in BoundedCuts (as compared to LocalCuts) the lowering comes at the expense of cutting more expensive edges. This increases the average performance ratio.

Avg. Performance Ratio

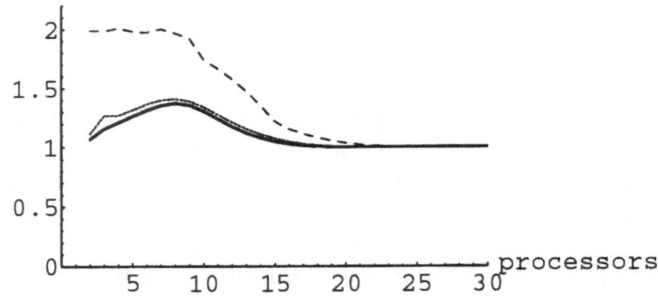

Fig. 4.11. Performance of Hybrid (Solid), BalancedFragments (Dotted) and Modified LPT (Dashed) on Narrow Trees

The second observation is that Hybrid outperforms the other two algorithms. We also note that while we could prove worst-case bounds on the performance ratio of Hybrid only for stars and paths, we do not know of any examples on which Hybrid has a performance ratio of more than 2.

Avg. Performance Ratio

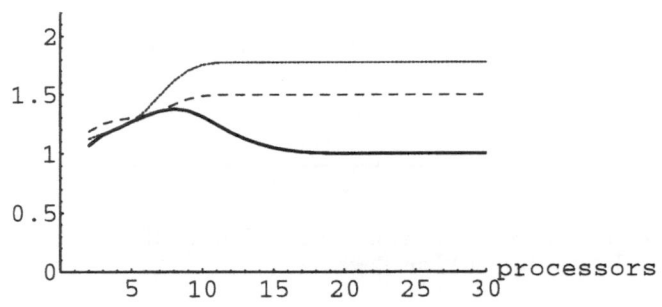

Fig. 4.12. Comparison of Hybrid (Solid), LocalCuts (Dashed) and BoundedCuts (Dotted) on Narrow Trees

4.8.5 Behavior of Lower Bound

Computing the optimal schedule even for a single tree is prohibitively expensive when the trees get large. In our implementation, it took a few days to compute the optimal schedule for a tree with 15 nodes. All reported performance ratio are therefore with respect to a lower bound on the optimal.

Avg. Performance Ratio

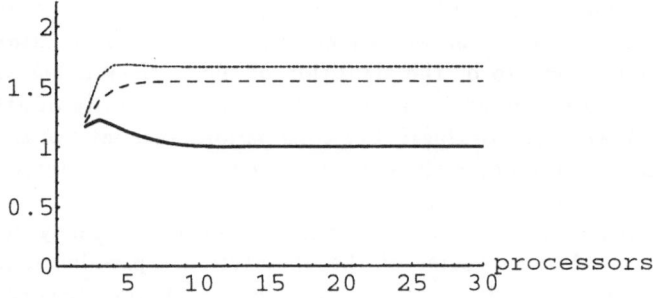

Fig. 4.13. Comparison of Hybrid (Solid), LocalCuts (Dashed) and BoundedCuts (Dotted) on Wide Trees

Figure 4.8.5 plot the performance ratio of the optimal (i.e. optimal response time divided by lower bound) for trees with 10 nodes and compares it with the performance ratio of Hybrid.

We observe that a reason for the humped nature of all curves is that the lower bound itself follows this pattern. When the number of nodes far exceeds the number of processors, the average node weight tends to be a good lower bound. When the number of node is almost the same as the number of processors, the maximum net weight is a good lower bound. The lower bounds are not as good in the intermediate region.

Avg. Performance Ratio

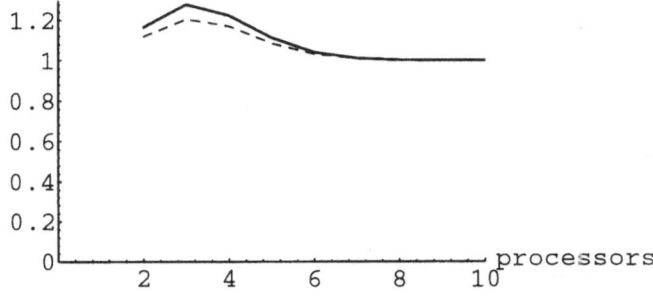

Fig. 4.14. Performance of Optimal (Dotted) and Hybrid (Solid)

4.9 Discussion

We developed several algorithms for managing pipelined parallelism and evaluated their average as well as worst-case performance ratios. Of these, we consider *Hybrid* to be the algorithm of choice since it has the best average performance ratio and a worst-case performance ratio of about 2 for many cases. We conjecture *Hybrid* to have a performance ratio of about 2 in general.

Some of the other algorithms developed in this chapter have properties that are worth discussing.

GreedyPairing has the advantage of being extremely simple. It is also easily usable when some of the operators are pre-allocated to processors. This is important in architectures where a disk may be scanned only by the processor that "owns" it.

Connected schedules have the practical advantage that certain code generation schemes (such as in LDL [CGK90]) can generate code with a *single* thread of control for a connected sets of operators. The context switching between operators is efficiently built into the generated code rather than being managed by more expensive mechanisms such as thread packages. Unconnected sets require as many threads as the number of connected components in the set. Thus connected schedules permit a faster implementation of intra-processor context switching.

LocalCuts and *BoundedCuts* have the advantage providing a guarantee on the worst-case performance ratio. We experimented with variations of *LocalCuts* such as the use of multiple values of α and trying out multiple choices of the root. Such variations improve average performance bringing is closer to the performance of *Hybrid*.

5. Scheduling Mixed Parallelism

In this chapter, we address the problem of scheduling a pipelined tree using both pipelined and partitioned parallelism. This problem is the continuous version of the discrete optimization problem addressed in the last chapter. When using only pipelined parallelism, each operator is allocated to a unique processor (a 0/1 assignment). Partitioned parallelism permits an operator to be allocated to a set of processors. Each processor executes some *fraction* of the operator.

Allowing partitioned parallelism enlarges the space of schedules. Interestingly, the problem gets simplified for the case when communication has zero cost. However, when communication is considered, the problem becomes NP-hard and is a continuous optimization problem that does *not* fall into classes such as convex or quadratic programming.

After defining the model, we investigate two interesting classes of schedules. Balanced schedules put equal load on all processors and symmetric schedules that divide each operator equally over all processors. We develop characterizations of the optimal schedule. We also show a simple rule for optimally scheduling trees with two nodes.

5.1 Problem Definition

Definition 5.1.1. *A schedule is a $n \times p$ matrix A with entries $a_{ik} \geq 0$ such that $\sum_{1 \leq k \leq p} a_{ik} = 1$. The number a_{ik} is the fraction of operator i executed by processor k.*

To understand communication costs, suppose operator i produces a data stream that is consumed by operator j. Assuming uniform production, fraction a_{ik} of the data stream will be produced on processor k. Assuming uniform redistribution of tuples, fraction a_{jk} is consumed by the local clone of operator j and fraction $1 - a_{jk}$ by non-local clones (In the terminology of Chapter 3, we are focusing on the case where each node is of a different color). Thus, on processor k, operator i incurs a communication cost of $c_{ij}a_{ik}(1 - a_{jk})$ with operator j. Generalizing, the total communication cost (with all other operators) incurred by i on processor k is $\sum_{1 \leq j \leq n} a_{ik}(1 - a_{jk})c_{ij}$.

Definition 5.1.2. *The load L_k on processor k is*

$$L_k = \sum_{1 \leq i \leq n} a_{ik}t_i + \sum_{\substack{1 \leq i \leq n \\ 1 \leq j \leq n}} a_{ik}(1 - a_{jk})c_{ij}$$

We will use $L_k(A)$ to denote the load on processor k in schedule A.

The response time, L, of a schedule is derived by reasoning similar to that in the last chapter. The pipelining constraints force all operators in a pipeline to start simultaneously (time 0) and terminate simultaneously at time L. Letting f_{ik} be the fraction of operator i executed by processor k, the pipelining constraint is:

$$f_{ik} = \frac{1}{L}[t_i + \sum_j a_{ik}(1 - a_{jk})c_{ij}] \tag{5.1}$$

Since at least one processor must be fully utilized, we have:

$$\max_{1 \leq k \leq p} [\sum_{1 \leq i \leq n} f_{ik}] = 1$$

$$\Rightarrow \quad L = \max_{1 \leq k \leq p} [\sum_{1 \leq i \leq n} [t_i + \sum_j a_{ik}(1 - a_{jk})c_{ij}]] = \max_{1 \leq k \leq p} L_k$$

(using equation (5.1))

Example 5.1.1. Figure 5.1 shows an operator tree with 2 nodes scheduled on two processors. Taking the SCAN operator to be operator 1 and BUILD to be operator 2, the schedule being illustrated has $a_{11} = 3/4$, $a_{12} = 1/4$, and $a_{21} = a_{22} = 1/2$. Processor 1 is saturated and the schedule has response time 22.

We now state the POTP (Pipelined Operator Tree with Partitioning) scheduling problem as the following continuous optimization problem:

Input: Operator Tree $T = (V, E)$ with positive real weights t_i for each
          node $i \in V$ and c_{ij} for each edge $(i, j) \in E$; number of processors p
Output: $n \times p$ matrix A that minimizes $L = \max_{1 \leq k \leq p} L_k$ subject to
$$a_{ik} \geq 0 \qquad\qquad\qquad\qquad \text{for } 1 \leq i \leq n, \ \ 1 \leq k \leq p$$
$$\textstyle\sum_{1 \leq k \leq p} a_{ik} = 1 \qquad\qquad\quad\ \text{for } 1 \leq i \leq n$$

We first observe that Lemma 4.2.2 applies to POTP and $\overline{W} = W/p$ where $W = \sum_i t_i$ is a lower bound on the response time of any schedule. Since operators are now divisible, the lower bound given by Lemma 4.2.1 does not apply (as a counter-example, consider a tree consisting of a single node scheduled on two processors).

Lemma 5.1.1. *POTP is NP-complete.*

Proof. (Sketch) The problem is in NP since the response time of a schedule is easily computed. To see the problem to NP-hard, consider a path with $2n$ nodes in which alternate edges have weights ∞ and 0. Since edges with

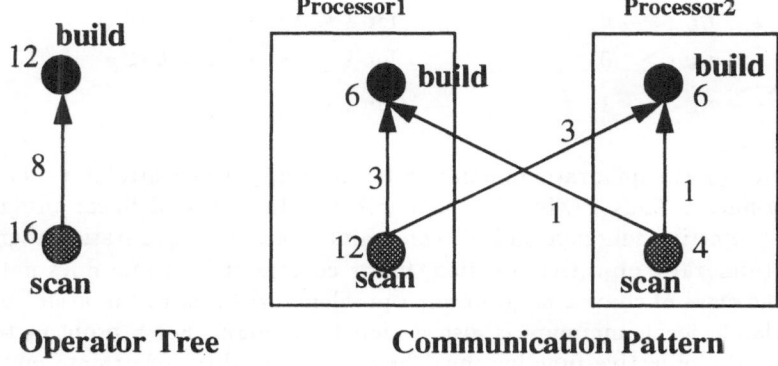

Operator Tree   **Communication Pattern**

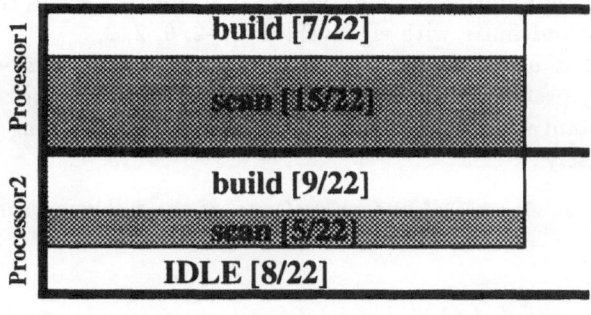

Gantt Chart

Fig. 5.1. Execution with Mixed Parallelism

∞ weight must be collapsed, the problem reduces classical Multiprocessor scheduling of the resulting n nodes and is thus NP-hard. In Section 5.2, we will show this proof idea to apply with finite edge weights.

Our formulation of POTP has an objective function that is not smooth due to the presence of max. Continuity of first and second derivatives is desirable in continuous analysis. The following equivalent formulation achieves smoothness:

Minimize z subject to

$$
\begin{aligned}
z - L_k &\geq 0 & \text{for } 1 \leq k \leq p \\
a_{ik} &\geq 0 & \text{for } 1 \leq i \leq n, \ 1 \leq k \leq p \\
\sum_{1 \leq k \leq p} a_{ik} &= 1 & \text{for } 1 \leq i \leq n
\end{aligned}
$$

Since L_k is a quadratic function in terms of a_{ik}, the constraint $z - L_k \geq 0$ is non-linear. Thus POTP does not fall into the class of linear programming (objective function and all constraints linear) or quadratic programming (quadratic objective function, linear constraints). It also does not fall into the class of convex programming problems which have the useful property that a local minimum is also a global minimum. For a problem to be convex, the objective function must be convex, equality constraints must be linear and inequality constraints must be convex. Unfortunately, the constraint $z - L_k \geq 0$ is neither convex nor concave due to its quadratic nature. This can be seen more formally by observing that for $n = p = 2$, the Hessian for $z - L_k \geq 0$ is indefinite with eigenvalues -2, -2, 0, 2, 2.

We will find it useful to distinguish between two schedules with equal response time by preferring the one that lowers load on some processors while keeping it constant on the remaining processors. The following definition states this precisely.

Definition 5.1.3. *$A < A'$ if and only if one of the following conditions is true:*

- $L(A) < L(A')$
- $L(A) = L(A')$ and $L_k(A) \leq L_k(A')$ for all processors k and there exists some processors k' such that $L_{k'}(A) < L_{k'}(A')$.

Two schedules are equal if neither is less than the other.

We will find it useful to reason with the partial derivatives of load functions.

$$
\frac{\partial L_k}{\partial a_{ik_1}} = \begin{cases} t_i + \sum_{1 \leq j \leq n}(1 - 2a_{jk})c_{ij} & \text{if } k_1 = k \\ 0 & \text{otherwise} \end{cases} \tag{5.2}
$$

$$
\frac{\partial^2 L_k}{\partial a_{ik_1} \partial a_{jk_2}} = \begin{cases} -2c_{ij} & \text{if } k = k_1 = k_2 \\ 0 & \text{otherwise} \end{cases} \tag{5.3}
$$

Definition 5.1.4. *We will use A_{ik} as a convenient notation for $\frac{\partial L_k}{\partial a_{ik}}$.*

5.2 Balanced Schedules

Definition 5.2.1. *A* balanced *schedule has equal load on all processors.*

In this section, we investigate properties of balanced schedules. This allows us to develop necessary conditions for minimal schedules. In particular, we will show that if a minimal schedule is not balanced then any processor k that has more load than some other processor must have $a_{ik} = 0$ or 1 for all operators i. Further, if S is the set of operators for which $a_{ik} = 1$, then $(\forall i \in S) t_i + \sum_{j \notin S} c_{ij} \le \sum_{j \in S} c_{ij}$.

Though scheduling in parallel systems is often termed "load balancing", the following example shows that there may be more than one balanced schedule and none of the balanced schedules may be optimal.

Example 5.2.1. Consider an operator tree with 2 nodes each of weight 1 and an edge of weight 4. If scheduled on two processors, the loads are:

$$L_1 = a_{11} + a_{21} + 4(a_{11}a_{22} + a_{21}a_{12})$$
$$L_2 = a_{12} + a_{22} + 4(a_{12}a_{21} + a_{22}a_{11})$$

The condition for a balanced schedule is $L_1 = L_2$ and may be simplified to yield $a_{11} + a_{21} = 1$. Thus, there are infinitely many balanced schedules. For example, the schedule with $a_{11} = a_{21} = 1/2$ is balanced and symmetrically divides each operator over all processors giving a response time of 3. Another balanced schedule is a pipelined schedule in which each operator is assigned to a different processor ($a_{11} = 1$ and $a_{21} = 0$) and has a response time of 5. The optimal schedule places both operators on the same processor to yield a response time of 2. (The optimality follows by Theorem 5.4.1 which is proved later in this chapter.)

Lemma 5.2.1. *Given an arbitrary schedule A and operator i, $A_{ik} \le 0$ for at most one processor k.*

Proof. We will assume $A_{ik} \le 0$ for two processors k_1 and k_2 and derive a contradiction. Using Definition 5.1.4, $A_{ik} \le 0$ may be written as $\frac{1}{2}(t_i + \sum_{1 \le j \le n} c_{ij}) \le \sum_{1 \le j \le n} a_{jk}c_{ij}$

$$A_{ik_1} + A_{ik_2} \le 0$$
$$\equiv t_i + \sum_{1 \le j \le n} c_{ij} \le \sum_{1 \le j \le n} (a_{jk_1} + a_{jk_2})c_{ij}$$

which is a contradiction since $a_{jk_1} + a_{jk_2} \le 1$ and $t_i > 0$.

Lemma 5.2.2. *For any local minima A, if $A_{ik} \le 0$ then $a_{ik} = 1$.*

Proof. Assuming $a_{ik} < 1$ in a locally minimal schedule A, we derive a' contradiction by showing the existence of neighboring schedule $A' < A$. If $a_{ik} < 1$, then there exists some processor k_1 such that $a_{ik_1} > 0$. We construct A' by increasing a_{ik} and decreasing a_{ik_1}. Since $A_{ik} \le 0$, by Lemma 5.2.1 $A_{ik_1} > 0$. Thus $A' < A$ since load is reduced on k_1 and does not increase on k.

Lemma 5.2.3. *Suppose locally minimal schedule A is not balanced and k_{max} is a processor with maximal load. Then for any operator i, either $a_{ik_{max}} = 1$ and $A_{ik_{max}} \leq 0$ or $a_{ik_{max}} = 0$ and $A_{ik_{max}} > 0$.*

$$\forall i[(a_{ik_{max}} = 1 \wedge A_{ik_{max}} \leq 0) \vee (a_{ik_{max}} = 0 \wedge A_{ik_{max}} > 0)]$$

Proof. For arbitrary operator i, we consider the cases $A_{ik_{max}} \leq 0$ and $A_{ik_{max}} > 0$.

If $A_{ik_{max}} \leq 0$ then by Lemma 5.2.1 we must have $A_{ik} > 0$ for all $k \neq k_{max}$. If $a_{ik_{max}} < 1$, then there must be some k_1 such that $a_{ik_1} > 0$ and $A_{ik_1} > 0$. We may reduce load on both k_{max} and k_1 by increasing $a_{ik_{max}}$ and decreasing a_{ik_1}. This contradicts the assumption of A being a local minima.

Now consider the case $A_{ik_{max}} > 0$. Since A is not balanced there must a processor k_{min} with strictly less load than k_{max}. If $a_{ik_{max}} > 0$, we may reduce the load on k_{max} by reducing $a_{ik_{max}}$ and increasing $a_{ik_{min}}$ (possibly increasing the load on k_{min}). The resulting schedule is less than A thus contradicting the assumption of A being a local minima.

Lemma 5.2.4. *If S is the set of operators on the bottleneck processor in an unbalanced local minima then each operator $i \in S$ satisfies*

$$t_i + \sum_{j \notin S} c_{ij} \leq \sum_{j \in S} c_{ij}$$

Proof. Letting k_{max} be the bottleneck processor, $i \in S$ if and only if $a_{ik_{max}} = 1$.

$$
\begin{aligned}
A_{ik_{max}} &= t_i + \sum_j (1 - 2a_{jk})c_{ij} \\
&= t_i + \sum_j c_{ij} - 2\sum_{j \in S} c_{ij} \\
&= t_i + \sum_{j \notin S} c_{ij} - \sum_{j \in S} c_{ij}
\end{aligned}
$$

Thus the condition $A_{ik_{max}} \leq 0$ may be written as $t_i + \sum_{j \notin S} c_{ij} \leq \sum_{j \in S} c_{ij}$

Lemmas 5.2.3 and 5.2.4 yield conditions that must be satisfied by the bottleneck processor in any unbalanced local minima. It is interesting to ask whether these lemmas can be applied recursively to the remaining processors.

Let P be some subset of the processors. Given schedule A for tree T, we may view the portion of the tree scheduled on subset P as a new tree T^P with schedule A^P. Tree T^P differs from T only in the values of the node and edge weights. Let α_{iP} be the total fraction of operator i on subset P.

Definition 5.2.2. *The projected tree T^P has node and edge weights given by*

$$t_i^P = t_i \alpha_{iP} + \sum_j \alpha_{iP} \alpha_{j\overline{P}} c_{ij}$$

$$c_{ij}^P = \alpha_{iP} \alpha_{jP} c_{ij}$$

$$\text{where } \alpha_{iP} = \sum_{k \in P} a_{ik}$$

The projected schedule A^P *has* $a_{ik}^P = a_{ik}/\alpha_{iP}$.

Given A to be a legal schedule, A^P is a legal schedule since $a_{ik}^P \geq 0$ and $\sum_{k \in P} a_{ik}^P = 1$. The following two Lemma establish that loads and strong minimality are invariant under projection.

Lemma 5.2.5. *The load on processor* $k \in P$ *under schedule* A^P *for tree* T^P *is identical to the load under schedule* A *for tree* T.

Proof. It suffices to show the load on processor k due to operator i to be identical under the two schedules.

$$a_{ik}^P t_i^P + \sum_j a_{ik}^P (1 - a_{jk}^P) c_{ij}^P$$

$$= \frac{a_{ik}}{\alpha_{iP}} [t_i \alpha_{iP} + \sum_j \alpha_{iP} \alpha_{j\overline{P}} c_{ij}] + \sum_j \frac{a_{ik}}{\alpha_{iP}} (1 - \frac{a_{jk}}{\alpha_{jP}}) \alpha_{iP} \alpha_{jP} c_{ij}$$

$$= a_{ik} t_i + \sum_j a_{ik} \alpha_{j\overline{P}} c_{ij} + \sum_j a_{ik} \alpha_{jP} c_{ij} - \sum_j a_{ik} a_{jk} c_{ij}$$

$$= a_{ik} t_i + \sum_j a_{ik} (1 - a_{jk}) c_{ij} \qquad \text{since } \alpha_{jP} + \alpha_{j\overline{P}} = 1$$

Local minimality comes in two forms: weak and strong. Strong minimality requires existence of a neighborhood in which all other schedules are *strictly* less than the minima. Weak minimality permits the neighboring schedules to have the same response time.

Strong minimality is retained by projection. Weak minimality may not be retained. For example, consider a neighbor A' of a weak minima A that keeps load constant on the bottleneck processor, increases load on the processor with second highest load and decreases it on some other processor. While $A' = A$, we have $A'^P < A^P$.

Lemma 5.2.6. *If* A *is a strong local minima for tree* T, *then* A^P *is a strong local minima for tree* T^P *where* P *is any subset of the processors.*

Thus, Lemma 5.2.3 and 5.2.4 may be applied recursively to unbalanced schedules that are strong local minima. This yields the structure illustrated in Figure 5.2. If S is the set of operators on any of the unbalanced processors, then each operator $i \in S$ satisfies $t_i + \sum_{j \notin S} c_{ij} \leq \sum_{j \in S} c_{ij}$.

A proof of Lemma 5.1.1, is given below (using Lemma 5.2.2):

Lemma 5.1.1 POTP is NP-complete.

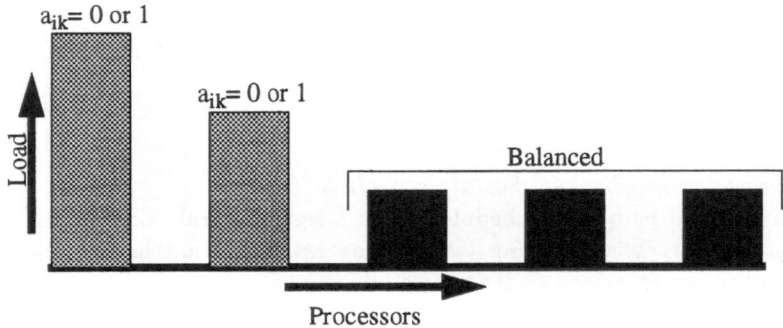

Fig. 5.2. Structure of (Strongly) Minimal Schedule

Proof. Given a path with alternate edges of weights c and 0, we show that the optimal must collapse all edges of weight c for large enough values of c. Let i and j be neighboring nodes connected by an edge of weight c.

We first consider the case $a_{ik}, a_{jk} \leq \delta$ for all k. The total communication incurred between i and j is

$$
\begin{aligned}
C_{ij} &= \sum_k a_{ik}(1 - a_{jk})c \\
&\geq c(1 - \delta) \sum_k a_{ik} = c(1 - \delta)
\end{aligned}
$$

Any schedule that incurs communication larger than $p \sum_i t_i$ cannot be optimal since we can form a better schedule by putting all operators on a single processor. Thus, a schedule with $a_{ik}, a_{jk} \leq \delta$ cannot be optimal if $c(1 - \delta) > p \sum_i t_i$ which may be written as $\delta < 1 - p \sum_i t_i/c$.

Now consider the other case: $a_{ik} > \delta$ for some i, k. Thus $A_{jk} = t_j + (1 - 2a_{ik})c$ and $A_{jk} < 0$ provided $a_{ik} > 1/2 + t_j/2c$. By Lemma 5.2.2, if $A_{jk} < 0$, then $a_{jk} = 1$. Thus $a_{jk} \geq a_{ik} > \delta$ and $a_{ik} = 1$ as well. Thus $a_{ik} > \delta > 1/2 + t_j/2c$ assures that nodes i and j will be collapsed in the optimal.

Combining the two cases, $1 - p \sum_i t_i/c > \delta > 1/2 + t_j/2c$ assures that all edges of weight c will be collapsed in the optimal. Such a value of δ can be found provided $c > 2p(\sum_i t_i) + max_i t_i$.

5.3 Symmetric Schedules

The symmetric schedule partitions each operator equally over all processors. In this section, we shall establish some properties of such schedules. We will show that symmetric schedules are optimal when communication is free. They are locally minimal for trees of size 2 but may not be locally minimal for larger trees. However, under extremely likely conditions, the symmetric schedule has the same response time as any interior local minima. Finally, symmetric schedules may be arbitrarily more expensive than the global minimum.

Definition 5.3.1. *The* symmetric schedule *has* $a_{ik} = \frac{1}{p}$ *for all operators* i, *processors* k.

The symmetric schedule has $L_k = \frac{\sum_i t_i}{p}$ when $c_{ij} = 0$. Thus $L = \frac{\sum_i t_i}{p}$ which is optimal since the lower bound of Lemma 4.2.2 is achieved.

Lemma 5.3.1. *The symmetric schedule is optimal when communication is free.*

However, when communication is not free, symmetric schedules may be arbitrarily sub-optimal. Consider a path with nodes of weight 1 and edges of weight c. For two processors, the symmetric schedule has a response time of $L = n/p + 2(p-1)(n-1)c/p^2$. If the path is long enough, the optimal schedule will chop the path into p pieces thus obtaining a response time of $L_{opt} = n/p + 2c$. When n/p is large L/L_{opt} goes to $1 + 2c$.

Lemma 5.3.2. *The symmetric schedule has an unbounded performance ratio when communication is not free.*

We will understand symmetric schedules further by investigating the Kuhn-Tucker conditions for local minima (see standard textbooks such as [GMW81, Lue89] for a review). Since symmetric schedules lie in the interior of the feasible space, it is useful to investigate the class of interior schedules.

Definition 5.3.2. *A schedule* A *is an* interior schedule *iff every processor is allocated a non-zero fraction of every operator i.e.* $0 < a_{ik} < 1$ *for all operators* i *and processors* k.

The following is a consequence of Lemmas 5.2.2 and 5.2.3.

Lemma 5.3.3. *If interior schedule* A *is a local minima, then* A *is a balanced schedule and* $A_{ik} > 0$ *for all operators* i, *processors* k.

The POTP problem is restated below. We will use $\mu_k \geq 0$, $\alpha_{ik} \geq 0$ and λ_i respectively as the Lagrange multipliers for the three kinds of constraints. In our use of matrices, we will treat the the variables in the order $z, a_{11}, \ldots, a_{1p}, a_{21}, \ldots, a_{22}, \ldots a_{n1}, \ldots, a_{np}$.

Minimize z
subject to

$$
\begin{aligned}
z - L_k &\geq 0 & &\text{for } 1 \leq k \leq p \\
a_{ik} &\geq 0 & &\text{for } 1 \leq i \leq n, \ 1 \leq k \leq p \\
\sum_{1 \leq k \leq p} a_{ik} &= 1 & &\text{for } 1 \leq i \leq n
\end{aligned}
$$

At an interior schedule, the constraint $a_{ik} \geq 0$ is not active and may be ignored. The Lagrangian function is therefore

$$L = z - \sum_k \mu_k(z - L_k) - \sum_i \lambda_i \left(\sum_k a_{ik} - 1 \right)$$

By the Kuhn-Tucker conditions, a minima can occur only at stationary points. A feasible point is said to be stationary if $\nabla L = 0$. The conditions for the z and a_{ik}'th components of ∇L to be zero are:

$$\sum_k \mu_k = 1 \tag{5.4}$$

$$-\mu_k A_{ik} + \lambda_i = 0 \qquad 1 \leq i \leq n \text{ and } 1 \leq k \leq p \tag{5.5}$$

Lemma 5.3.4. *The symmetric schedule is a stationary point.*

Proof. We need to show that the symmetric schedule is feasible and $\nabla L = 0$. Since $a_{ik} = \frac{1}{p}$, the constraints $a_{ik} \geq 0$ and $\sum_{1 \leq k \leq p} a_{ik} = 1$ are satisfied. For any processor k, $L_k = \sum_i \frac{1}{p} t_i + \sum_{ij} \frac{1}{p}(1 - \frac{1}{p}) c_{ij} = \frac{1}{p}[\sum_i t_i + \frac{p-1}{p} \sum_{ij} c_{ij}]$. Thus $z - L_k \geq 0$ is satisfied with $z = \frac{1}{p}[\sum_i t_i + \frac{p-1}{p} \sum_{ij} c_{ij}]$. This establishes the feasibility of the symmetric schedule.

Observe that $A_{ik} = t_i + \sum_j (1 - 2a_{jk}) c_{ij} = t_i + \frac{p-2}{p} \sum_j c_{ij}$ is independent of k. By Equation 5.5, this implies that μ_k is independent of k and Equation 5.4 gives $\mu_k = \frac{1}{p}$. It follows that $\lambda_i = pt_i + (p-2) \sum_j c_{ij}$. Thus the symmetric schedule satisfies $\nabla L = 0$ with $\mu_k = \frac{1}{p}$ and $\lambda_i = pt_i + (p-2) \sum_j c_{ij}$.

Lemma 5.3.5. *If interior schedule A is a stationary point then $\lambda_1, \ldots, \lambda_n$ and $\mu_1, \ldots, \mu_p$ are strictly positive.*

Proof. By Equation 5.5, $A_{ik} = \frac{\lambda_i}{\mu_k}$. Since $A_{ik} > 0$ by Lemma 5.3.3 and $\mu_k \geq 0$, we must have $\lambda_i > 0$ and $\mu_k > 0$.

We will now establish that for $n = 2$ and arbitrary p, the symmetric schedule is the only interior stationary point that could be a local minima (Lemma 5.3.6) and that it is indeed a local minima (Lemma 5.3.7)

Lemma 5.3.6. *For $n=2$ and arbitrary number of processors, the symmetric schedule is the only interior stationary point that may be a local minima.*

Proof. A local minima must satisfy Equation 5.4 and, by Lemma 5.3.3, must be balanced. We show that this permits exactly one solution, the symmetric schedule, for $n = 2$.

By Equation 5.5, $A_{ik} = \frac{\lambda_i}{\mu_k}$ at a stationary point. Using Definition 5.1.4, this may be rewritten as

$$\sum_j a_{jk} c_{ij} = \frac{1}{2}[t_i + \sum_j c_{ij} - \frac{\lambda_i}{\mu_k}]$$

Since $n = 2$, $\sum_j a_{jk} c_{ij} = a_{2k} c_{12}$ for $i = 1$ and $a_{1k} c_{12}$ for $i = 2$. Thus, for any fixed k,

$$a_{1k} = \frac{1}{2c_{12}}[t_2 + c_{12} - \frac{\lambda_2}{\mu_k}] \quad \text{and} \quad a_{2k} = \frac{1}{2c_{12}}[t_1 + c_{12} - \frac{\lambda_1}{\mu_k}] \quad (5.6)$$

The load on processor k is derived as follows. Equation 5.7 is obtained by substituting (5.6) and simplifying.

$$\begin{aligned} L_k &= \sum_i a_{ik} t_i + \sum_{i,j} a_{ik}(1 - a_{jk}) c_{ij} \\ &= a_{1k} t_1 + a_{2k} t_2 + (a_{1k} + a_{2k}) c_{12} - 2 a_{1k} a_{2k} c_{12} \\ &= \frac{t_1 t_2}{2 c_{12}} + \frac{t_1 + t_2 + c_{12}}{2} - \frac{\lambda_1 \lambda_2}{2 c_{12} \mu_k{}^2} \end{aligned} \quad (5.7)$$

By Lemma 5.3.3, an interior local minima is balanced and thus L_k is independent of k. Given (5.7), this requires μ_k^2 to be independent of k. By Lemma 5.3.5, $\mu_k > 0$ and thus μ_k is independent of k.

From Equations (5.6) it follows that the values of a_{1k} and a_{2k} must be independent of k. Thus the symmetric schedule is the only possible solution.

Lemma 5.3.7. *For n=2 and arbitrary number of processors, the symmetric schedule is a local minima.*

Proof. Lemma 5.3.4 established the symmetric schedule to be a stationary point and Lemma 5.3.5 showed the Lagrange multipliers to be positive at any stationary point. Thus it suffices to show the projected Hessian of the Lagrangian function to be positive definite.

We will establish $Z^T W Z$ be positive definite where $W = (G - \sum_t f_t G_t)$ is the Hessian of the Lagrangian function (G_t is the Hessian and f_t the Lagrange multiplier for the t'th constraint, G is the Hessian for the objective function) and Z is a matrix whose columns form a basis for the null space of A, the Jacobian matrix of the constraints. We first give the proof for $p = 2$ and then generalize.

[PROOF FOR $n = p = 2$]

Our optimization problem for $n = p = 2$ is:

Minimize z

subject to

$$\begin{aligned} z - L_1 &\geq 0 \\ z - L_2 &\geq 0 \\ a_{11} + a_{12} &= 1 \\ a_{21} + a_{22} &= 1 \end{aligned}$$

Since $A_{ik} = \frac{\lambda_i}{\mu_k}$ by Equation 5.5, the Jacobian of the constraints may be written as (our convention is to list variables in the order $z, a_{11}, a_{12}, a_{21}, a_{22}$):

$$A = \begin{bmatrix} 1 & -\frac{\lambda_1}{\mu_1} & 0 & -\frac{\lambda_2}{\mu_1} & 0 \\ 1 & 0 & -\frac{\lambda_1}{\mu_2} & 0 & -\frac{\lambda_2}{\mu_2} \\ 0 & 1 & 1 & 0 & 0 \\ 0 & 0 & 0 & 1 & 1 \end{bmatrix}$$

The matrix Z whose columns form a basis for the null space of A is $Z = [0 \quad \lambda_2 \quad -\lambda_2 \quad -\lambda_1 \quad \lambda_1]^T$. Since the objective function and the last two constraints are linear, $G = G_{\lambda_1} = G_{\lambda_2} = 0$. From Equation 5.3, $\frac{\partial^2 L_k}{\partial a_{ik} \partial a_{jk}} = -2c_{ij}$ is independent of k and thus G_{μ_1} and G_{μ_2} are equal. Since $\mu_1 + \mu_2 = 1$ by (5.4), we have $\mu_1 G_{\mu_1} + \mu_2 G_{\mu_2} = G_{\mu_1}$ which yields $W = -G_{\mu_1}$. Since $c_{ii} = 0$, we have:

$$W = -G_{\mu_1} = \begin{bmatrix} 0 & 0 & 0 & 0 & 0 \\ 0 & 0 & 0 & -2c_{12} & 0 \\ 0 & 0 & 0 & 0 & -2c_{12} \\ 0 & -2c_{12} & 0 & 0 & 0 \\ 0 & 0 & -2c_{12} & 0 & 0 \end{bmatrix}$$

Multiplying out $Z^T W Z$ yields the 1×1 matrix $8\lambda_1\lambda_2 c_{12}$. Thus the only eigenvalue is $8\lambda_1\lambda_2 c_{12}$ which is positive since $\lambda_1, \lambda_2 > 0$ by Lemma 5.3.5.

[PROOF FOR $n = 2$, p ARBITRARY]

We now sketch how the proof generalizes for arbitrary p. (Figure 5.3 illustrates the values of some of the matrices for $p = 3$).

The matrix A has a simpler form if we multiply the row for $z - L_k$ by μ_k. The matrix A is the following $(p + 2) \times (2p + 1)$ matrix in which I is a $p \times p$ identity matrix.

$$A = \begin{bmatrix} \mu_1 & & & \\ \mu_2 & & & \\ \vdots & -\lambda_1 I & -\lambda_2 I \\ \mu_p & & & \\ 0 & 1 \ldots 1 & 0 \ldots 0 \\ 0 & 0 \ldots 0 & 1 \ldots 1 \end{bmatrix}$$

The null space of A is the following $(2p + 1) \times (p - 1)$ matrix Z. The sub-matrix R is a $p \times (p-1)$ matrix in which all elements of the first row are 1. The bottom-left to top-right diagonal of the remaining $(p - 1) \times (p - 1)$ matrix consists of -1's and the remaining elements are zero.

$$Z = \begin{bmatrix} 0 \ldots 0 \\ \lambda_2 R \\ -\lambda_1 R \end{bmatrix}$$

The matrix W has the value $-G_{\mu_1}$ by reasoning similar to the case $p = 2$ and is the following $(2p + 1) \times (2p + 1)$ matrix where I is the $p \times p$ identity matrix and 0 is the $p \times p$ matrix of zeros.

$$A = \begin{bmatrix} \mu_1 & -\lambda_1 & 0 & 0 & -\lambda_2 & 0 & 0 \\ \mu_2 & 0 & -\lambda_1 & 0 & 0 & -\lambda_2 & 0 \\ \mu_3 & 0 & 0 & -\lambda_1 & 0 & 0 & -\lambda_2 \\ 0 & 1 & 1 & 1 & 0 & 0 & 0 \\ 0 & 0 & 0 & 0 & 1 & 1 & 1 \end{bmatrix}$$

$$Z = \begin{bmatrix} 0 & 0 \\ \lambda_2 & \lambda_2 \\ 0 & -\lambda_2 \\ -\lambda_2 & 0 \\ -\lambda_1 & -\lambda_1 \\ 0 & \lambda_1 \\ \lambda_1 & 0 \end{bmatrix}$$

$$W = \begin{bmatrix} 0 & 0 & 0 & 0 & 0 & 0 & 0 \\ 0 & 0 & 0 & 0 & -2c_{12} & 0 & 0 \\ 0 & 0 & 0 & 0 & 0 & -2c_{12} & 0 \\ 0 & 0 & 0 & 0 & 0 & 0 & -2c_{12} \\ 0 & -2c_{12} & 0 & 0 & 0 & 0 & 0 \\ 0 & 0 & -2c_{12} & 0 & 0 & 0 & 0 \\ 0 & 0 & 0 & -2c_{12} & 0 & 0 & 0 \end{bmatrix}$$

$$X = \begin{bmatrix} 2 & 1 \\ 1 & 2 \end{bmatrix}$$

Fig. 5.3. Matrices for $p = 3$

$$W = \begin{bmatrix} \begin{matrix} 0 \\ 0 \\ \vdots \\ 0 \end{matrix} & \begin{matrix} 0 \dots 0 \\ \\ 0 \\ \\ \end{matrix} & \begin{matrix} 0 \dots 0 \\ \\ -2c_{12}I \\ \\ \end{matrix} \\ \begin{matrix} 0 \\ \vdots \\ 0 \end{matrix} & -2c_{12}I & 0 \end{bmatrix}$$

Multiplying out $Z^T W Z$ yields $4c_{12}\lambda_1\lambda_2 X$ where X is a $(p-1) \times (p-1)$ matrix in which the diagonal entries are 2 and the remaining entries are 1. The determinant of $X - \beta I$ may be shown to be $(\beta - p)(\beta - 1)^{p-2}$. Thus X has only positive eigenvalues and is positive definite.

Lemma 5.3.8. *If a tree contains a mother node m with distinct leaf children s and d s.t. $\frac{t_s}{c_{ms}} \neq \frac{t_d}{c_{md}}$ then, for any number of processors, any interior minima has the same response time as the symmetric schedule.*

Proof. A local minima must satisfy Equations 5.4 and 5.5 and by Lemma 5.3.3 must be balanced. We show, given $\frac{t_s}{c_{ms}} \neq \frac{t_d}{c_{md}}$, these conditions imply that all interior minima have the same response time as the symmetric schedule.

We first use $\frac{t_s}{c_{ms}} \neq \frac{t_d}{c_{md}}$ and Equations 5.4,5.5 to show $\mu_k = 1/p$. We then show $\sum_j a_{jk}c_{ij}$ to have a value independent of k and use it to show the total communication cost at any interior stationary point to equal that of the symmetric schedule. Since an interior local minima is balanced, we may the response time of any interior minima to equal the symmetric schedule.

By Equation 5.4, $A_{ik} = \frac{\lambda_i}{\mu_k}$ at a stationary point. Using Definition 5.1.4, this may be rewritten as

$$2\sum_j a_{jk}c_{ij} = t_i + \sum_j c_{ij} - \frac{\lambda_i}{\mu_k} \tag{5.8}$$

Taking $i = d$ and noting that the only neighbor of d is m, we obtain

$$2a_{mk}c_{md} = t_d + c_{md} - \frac{\lambda_d}{\mu_k} \tag{5.9}$$

$$\Rightarrow \quad 2c_{md} = p(t_d + c_{md}) - \lambda_d \sum_k \frac{1}{\mu_k} \qquad \text{summing over } k$$

$$\Rightarrow \quad \lambda_d = (pt_d + (p-2)c_{md}) / \sum_l \frac{1}{\mu_l} \tag{5.10}$$

rearranging and renaming k to l

Substituting back in Equation 5.9 and rearranging

$$2a_{mk} = \frac{t_d}{c_{md}}[1 - \frac{p}{\mu_k \sum_l 1/\mu_l}] + 1 - \frac{p-2}{\mu_k \sum_l 1/\mu_l}$$

A similar derivation for $i = s$ leads to another expression for a_{mk}.

$$2a_{mk} = \frac{t_s}{c_{ms}}[1 - \frac{p}{\mu_k \sum_l 1/\mu_l}] + 1 - \frac{p-2}{\mu_k \sum_l 1/\mu_l}$$

Since $\frac{t_s}{c_{ms}} \neq \frac{t_d}{c_{md}}$, the above equations are consistent only under the condition $1 - p/[\mu_k \sum_l 1/\mu_l] = 0$ or

$$\mu_k \sum_l 1/\mu_l = p \qquad\qquad (5.11)$$

$$\Rightarrow \quad (\sum_k \mu_k) \sum_l 1/\mu_l = p^2 \qquad \text{summing over } k$$

$$\Rightarrow \quad \sum_l 1/\mu_l = p^2 \qquad \text{using Equation 5.4}$$

$$\Rightarrow \quad \mu_k = 1/p \qquad \text{substituting back in 5.11}$$

We now show that $\mu_k = 1/p$ implies $\sum_j a_{jk}c_{ij} = 1/p \sum_j c_{ij}$. Substituting $\mu_k = 1/p$ in Equation 5.8

$$p\lambda_i = t_i + \sum_j (1 - 2a_{jk})c_{ij} \qquad\qquad (5.12)$$

$$\Rightarrow \quad p^2 \lambda_i = pt_i + (p-2) \sum_j c_{ij} \qquad \text{summing over } k$$

$$\Rightarrow \quad \lambda_i = \frac{t_i}{p} + \frac{(p-2)}{p^2} \sum_j c_{ij} \qquad\qquad (5.13)$$

Substituting the value of λ_i in Equation 5.12 and simplifying gives

$$\sum_j a_{jk}c_{ij} = \frac{1}{p} \sum_j c_{ij} \qquad\qquad (5.14)$$

We now show that the communication cost to be the same at each stationary point. The total communication cost of a schedule is $\sum_{i,j,k} a_{ik}(1 - a_{jk})c_{ij}$ which is $\sum_{i,j} c_{ij} - \sum_{i,j,k} a_{ik}a_{jk}c_{ij}$.

$$\sum_{i,j,k} a_{ik}a_{jk}c_{ij} = \sum_{i,k} a_{ik} \sum_j a_{jk}c_{ij}$$

$$= \sum_{i,k} a_{ik} \frac{1}{p} \sum_j c_{ij} \qquad \text{applying Equation 5.14}$$

$$= \frac{1}{p} \sum_{j,k} \sum_i a_{ik}c_{ij}$$

$$= \frac{1}{p^2} \sum_{j,k} \sum_i c_{ij} \qquad \text{applying Equation 5.14}$$

$$= \frac{1}{p} \sum_{i,j} c_{ij}$$

The total communication cost is therefore $\frac{p-1}{p}\sum_{i,j}c_{ij}$ which is equal to the communication cost of the symmetric schedule.

By Lemma 5.3.3 an interior minima is balanced. It follows that the response time of any interior minima equals that of the symmetric schedule.

It is worth observing that the set of equations 5.14 along with the constraint $\sum_k a_{ik} = 1$ has solutions other than the symmetric schedule. For example for $n = 3$, $p = 2$ any solution of the $a_{11} = a_{12} = 1/2$; $a_{21} = \frac{1}{2}+dc_{13}/c_{12}$; $a_{22} = \frac{1}{2} - dc_{13}/c_{12}$; $a_{31} = \frac{1}{2} - d$; $a_{22} = \frac{1}{2} + d$; is a solution for any $0 \le d \le \min(\frac{1}{2}c_{12}/c_{13})$.

Lemma 5.3.9. *The symmetric schedule may not be a local minima.*

Proof. **(Counter-Example)**
Consider the tree shown in Figure 5.4 to be scheduled on two processors. Observing that $c_{13} = 0$, the load on processor 1 is given by:

$$
\begin{aligned}
L_1 &= a_{11}t_1 + a_{21}t_2 + a_{31}t_3 + a_{11}(1 - a_{21})c_{12} + a_{21}(1 - a_{11})c_{12} \\
&= a_{11} + a_{21} + 2a_{31} + c_{12}(a_{11} + a_{21} - 2a_{11}a_{21})
\end{aligned}
$$

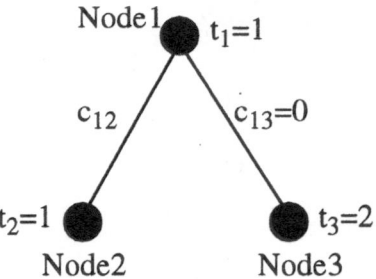

Fig. 5.4. Counter-Example: Tree for Which Symmetric Schedule is a Saddle Point

Noting that for two processors, $a_{i2} = 1 - a_{i1}$ and equal communication is incurred by both processors

$$
\begin{aligned}
L_2 &= (1 - a_{11})t_1 + (1 - a_{21})t_2 + (1 - a_{31})t_3 + c_{12}(a_{11} + a_{21} - 2a_{11}a_{21}) \\
&= 4 - a_{11} - a_{21} - 2a_{31} + c_{12}(a_{11} + a_{21} - 2a_{11}a_{21})
\end{aligned}
$$

The condition for a balanced schedule is $L_1 = L_2$ which gives $a_{11} + a_{21} + 2a_{31} = 2$. The response time of a balanced schedule is given by the load on any processor which we may now write as:

$$
\begin{aligned}
L_1 &= a_{11} + a_{21} + 2a_{31} + c_{12}(a_{11} + a_{21} - 2a_{11}a_{21}) \\
&= 2 + c_{12}(a_{11} + a_{21} - 2a_{11}a_{21})
\end{aligned}
$$

Figure 5.5 shows a plot of the function $z = a_{11} + a_{21} - 2a_{11}a_{21}$ that makes it clear that the symmetric schedule is a saddle-point.

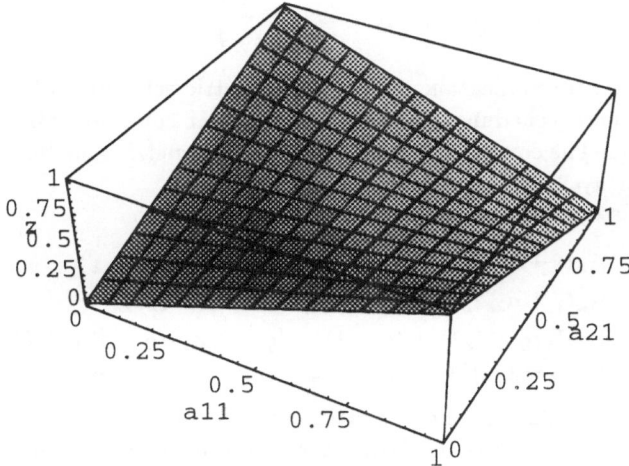

Fig. 5.5. Plot of $z = a_{11} + a_{21} - 2a_{11}a_{21}$ with a_{11} on x-Axis, a_{21} on y-Axis

5.4 Scheduling Trees with Two Nodes

We will now establish the following theorem that shows that tree with two nodes may be scheduled optimally by a simple method. The proof is based on the two lemmas presented below.

Theorem 5.4.1. *For n=2, the optimal schedule is either the symmetric schedule or a schedule that computes the entire tree on a single processor.*

Lemma 5.4.1. *For n=2, any balanced schedule A in which processors $Q = \{1, \ldots, q\}$ compute both operators and $Q_1 = \{q+1, \ldots, p\}$ compute only operator 1 is either not a local minima or no better than the symmetric schedule.*

Proof. Figure 5.6 illustrates the assumptions of the Lemma (such schedules may be termed one-sided). We will show A to be inferior to the symmetric schedule for $q \geq 2$ and to be not a local minima for $q = 1$.

Since A is a local minima A_Q must also be a local minima (Lemma 5.2.5). Clearly A_Q is an interior schedule and thus (by Lemmas 5.3.6 and 5.3.7) must be the symmetric schedule. This implies (by Definition 5.2.2) that a_{ik} is independent of k for $k \in Q$. Since each processor $k \in Q_1$ computes only operator 1 and processor loads are balanced, a_{ik} is independent of k for $k \in Q_1$.

If a is the total fraction of operator 1 on Q, $a_{1k} = a/q, a_{2k} = 1/q$ for $k \in Q$ and $a_{1k} = (1-a)/(p-q), a_{2k} = 0$ for $k \in Q_1$. The total communication, C, in schedule A is

$$C = \sum_k [a_{1k}(1 - a_{2k})c_{12} + a_{2k}(1 - a_{1k})c_{12}]$$

$$= \ 2c_{12} - 2c_{12} \sum_{k} a_{1k}a_{2k} = 2c_{12} - \frac{2ac_{12}}{q}$$

Similarly, the communication cost of a symmetric schedule is $2c_{12} - 2c_{12}/p$. Among balanced schedule, a schedule with lower communication has lower response time. The condition for A to beat the symmetric schedule is therefore $a/q > 1/p$ or $a_{1k} > 1/p$ for $k \in Q$.

The loads on processors are:

$$
\begin{aligned}
L_k \ &= \ a_{1k}t_1 + a_{2k}t_2 + a_{1k}(1 - a_{2k})c_{12} + a_{2k}(1 - a_{1k})c_{12} \\
&= \ a_{1k}t_1 + a_{2k}t_2 + (a_{1k} + a_{2k})c_{12} - 2a_{1k}a_{2k}c_{12} \\
&= \ \begin{cases} at_1/q + t_2/q + (a+1)c_{12}/q - 2ac_{12}/q^2 & \text{if } k \in Q \\ (t_2 + c_{12})(1 - a)/(p - q) & \text{if } k \in Q_1 \end{cases}
\end{aligned}
$$

Since $a/q > 1/p$ may be rewritten as $(1 - a)/(p - q) < 1/p$, we have $L_k < (t_2 + c_{12})/p$ for $k \in Q_1$. Using the equation for $k \in Q$, we may derive $L_k \geq (t_2 + c_{12})/q + ac_{12}/q[1 - 2/q]$. Thus the schedule is *not* balanced provided $q \geq 2$.

We now show that if $q = 1$, then the schedule is not a local minima. We will show that A_{1k} is negative for $k = 1$ and positive for $k > 1$. Thus we cannot have a local minima since the load on all processors may be reduced by increasing a.

Now, $A_{11} = t_1 + (1 - 2a_{21})c_{12} = t_1 - c$. We observe the condition for balanced loads for $q = 1$ is

$$at_1 + t_2 + (a+1)c_{12} - 2ac_{12} = (t_2 + c_{12})(1 - a)/(p - 1)$$
$$\equiv (t_2 + c_{12}) + a(t_1 - c_{12}) = (t_2 + c_{12})(1 - a)/(p - 1)$$

Since $(1 - a)/(p - 1) < 1$, we may conclude $t_1 - c_{12} < 0$. For $k > 1$, we have $A_{1k} = t_1 + (1 - 2a_{2k})c_{12} = t_2 + (p - 2 + a)/(p - 1)$ which is clearly positive since $p \geq 2$.

Lemma 5.4.2. *For n=2, any balanced schedule is either not a local minima or no better than the symmetric schedule.*

Proof. We will assume A to be a balanced local minima and argue it to be no better than the symmetric schedule. A balanced schedule for a tree with two nodes has the structure shown in Figure 5.7 where the load on all processors is identical. The set of processors Q compute both operators, Q_1 computes only operator 1, and Q_2 computes only operator 2. Applying Lemma 5.4.1 twice completes the proof.

5.5 Discussion

We have developed a model for exploiting both pipelined and partitioned parallelism. We investigated the classes balanced and symmetric schedules.

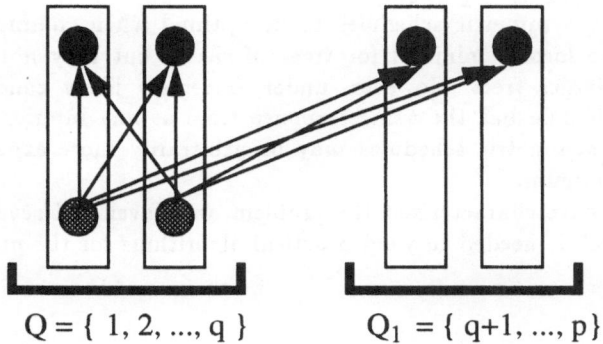

Fig. 5.6. One Sided Schedule

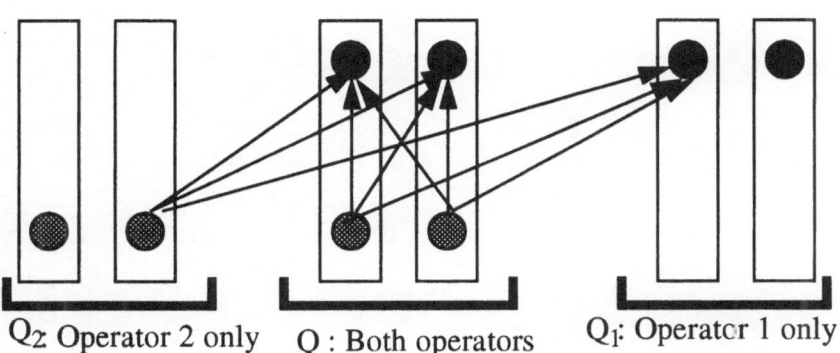

Fig. 5.7. Balanced Schedule for n=2 (Some Communication Arcs omitted)

We showed that there may be more than one balanced schedule and none of the balanced schedules may be optimal. We characterized the structure of optimal schedules. If a minimal schedule is not balanced then any processor k that has more load than some other processor must have $a_{ik} = 0$ or 1 for all operators i. Further, if S is the set of operators for which $a_{ik} = 1$, then $(\forall i \in S)t_i + \sum_{j \notin S} c_{ij} \leq \sum_{j \in S} c_{ij}$.

We showed symmetric schedules to be optimal when communication is free. They are locally minimal for trees of size 2 but may not be locally minimal for larger trees. However, under extremely likely conditions, the symmetric schedule has the same response time as any interior local minima. Finally, symmetric schedules may be arbitrarily more expensive than the global minimum.

While we have characterized the problem and developed several results, further research is needed to yield practical algorithms for the problem.

6. Summary and Future Work

In this chapter, we summarize our contributions and discuss some directions for future work[1].

6.1 Summary of Contributions

In this thesis we have addressed the problem of optimizing SQL queries for parallel machines. Exploiting parallel machines has led to new query processing strategies based on exploiting several forms of parallel execution. Further, the decreasing cost of computing motivates minimizing the response time to produce the query result as opposed to the traditional practice of minimizing the machine resources (work) consumed in answering the query. The problem of finding the best procedural plan for a declarative query poses fresh challenges since we are dealing with a new space of procedural plans as well as a new optimization objective.

The response time of a query may be reduced by two complementary tactics, reducing total work and partitioning work among processors. Partitioning work among processors may not yield ideal speedup due to two obstacles. First, timing constraints between operators and data placement constraints place intrinsic limits on available parallelism. It may become impossible to partition work equally over all processors thus reducing the speedup from parallel execution. Second, partitioning work generates extra work due to the resulting need to communicate data across processors. This may reduce or even offset the benefit from exploiting parallel execution.

Our two-phase architecture (Figure 6.1) for parallel query optimization is a refinement of ideas due to Hong and Stonebraker [HS91, Hon92b]. We apply the two tactics for reducing response time as two phases. The first phase, JOQR (for Join Ordering and Query Rewrite), minimizes total work while the second phase, parallelization, partitions work among processors. Breakup into phases provides a way of conquering problem complexity. It eases the understanding of problems as well as the development of solutions.

---

[1] Parts of this chapter have also been published as the paper *W. Hasan, D. Florescu and P. Valduriez: Open Issues in Parallel Query Optimization, Sigmod Record, Sep 1996*

We started with a performance study to understand how use of parallel execution can result in the generation of extra work. The study was conducted on NonStop SQL/MP, a commercial parallel database system from Tandem Computers. Since a query is executed in parallel by a set of cooperating processes, we measured two kinds of overhead costs of parallel execution, startup and communication. Startup consists of obtaining and initializing the processes. Communication consists of data transfer among processes. Our experiments led to three findings: First, startup costs become negligible when processes are reused rather than created afresh. Second, communication cost consists of the CPU cost of sending and receiving messages. Third, communication costs can exceed the cost of operators such as scanning, joining or grouping.

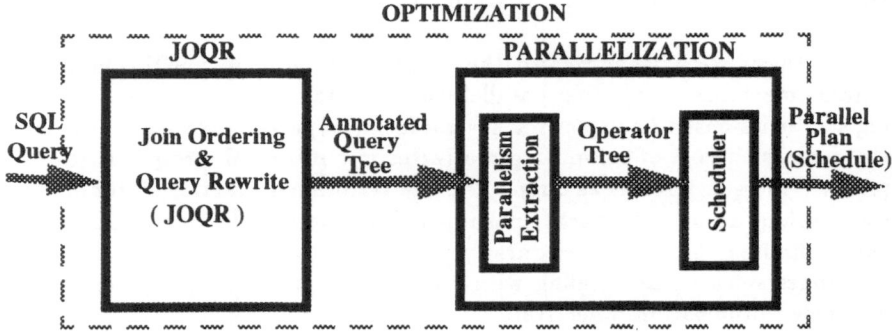

Fig. 6.1. Phases and Sub-phases of Parallel Query Optimization

One conclusion from our experiments is that startup costs can be effectively controlled by modifying a query execution system to reuse processes rather than creating them afresh. Communications costs, on the other hand, appear endemic to parallel execution. Machine architecture changes, such as offloading communication to specialized processors, hold the possibility of reducing communication costs. However, much of CPU cost of communication is incurred by software layers above the communication layer and will therefore still be substantial. This is a consequence of the low levels of abstraction offered by communication layers due to the need to cater to many different applications. We therefore concluded that query optimization should be based on models that incorporate the cost of communication but omit the cost of startup.

In Chapter 3, we developed algorithms for a series of increasingly sophisticated models for the JOQR phase. We started by posing the minimization of communication costs as a tree coloring problem (related to the Multiway

Cut [DJP+92] problem) where colors represent data partitioning. We then enhanced the model by two generalizations. The first generalization was to capture the interaction of computation and communication costs by supporting a set of alternate methods for each operator. The cost of a method can be an arbitrary function of the color and statistical properties of the inputs. Each method has an input-output constraint that provides guarantees on the color of the output as a function of colors of the inputs. The second generalization was based on the observation that communication may be viewed as resulting from changing the physical location of data. Since other physical properties of data such as sort-order or the existence of an index also impact the cost of a method, we generalized colors to represent collections of physical properties. The final enhancement of the model was to permit joins to be reordered.

Our work on the JOQR phase shows that optimally exploiting physical properties may be separated from join ordering. The separation has some advantages. Firstly, we showed that physical property optimization may be achieved by a fast polynomial algorithm. In contrast, only exponential algorithms are known for optimal ordering of joins. Secondly, physical property optimization is not limited to SPJ queries, it applies as well to query trees that contain operators such as grouping and foreign functions. Thirdly, we open up alternate ways of combining physical property optimization with join ordering. Another contribution of our work is an explanation and formalization of the basic ideas used in existing commercial query optimizers.

After addressing problems in the JOQR phase, we moved on to the problems in the parallelization phase. We addressed the problem of POT (pipelined operator tree) scheduling which is to exploit pipelined parallelism for operator trees with only pipelining edges. Our model of response time captured the fundamental tradeoff between parallel execution and its communication overhead. We assessed the quality of a scheduling algorithm by its performance ratio which is the ratio of the response time of the generated schedule to that of the optimal. We developed worst-case bounds on the performance ratio by analytical methods and measured the average performance ratios by use of experimental benchmarks. Of the several algorithms developed, we consider *Hybrid* to be the algorithm of choice since it has the best average performance ratio and a worst-case performance ratio of about 2 for many cases.

Our work on POT scheduling has several aspects that are interesting in their own right. We developed the notion of worthless parallelism which is parallelism that is never beneficial. Such parallelism may be efficiently removed from operator trees to yield a subclass of operator trees that we term monotone. Monotone trees have an additional lower bound that proved useful in analyzing the performance ratio of algorithms. We showed that the optimal connected schedules may be found by an efficient polynomial-time algorithm. Connected schedules have the practical advantage that certain code generation schemes can generate code with a single thread of control for a connected sets of operators. The context switching between operators is efficiently built into the generated code rather than being managed by more expensive mechanisms such as thread packages.

The algorithms that "lost" to *Hybrid* have features that make them useful. The *GreedyPairing* algorithm has the advantage of being extremely simple. It is also easily usable when data placement constraints pre-allocate some of the operators to specific processors. While we could prove the worst-case performance ratios of *Hybrid* and *GreedyPairing* for some cases, we could not prove or find counter-examples for the remaining cases. On the other hand, the *LocalCuts* and *BoundedCuts* algorithms have the advantage providing a guarantee on the worst-case performance ratio.

The last problem addressed in this thesis is the POTP (pipelined operator tree with partitioning) problem of exploiting both pipelined and partitioned parallelism in scheduling a pipelined operator tree. POTP is the continuous version of POT scheduling since partitioned parallelism permits several processors to each execute some fraction of an operator. POTP expands the class of permissible schedules as compared to POT. One effect of this expansion is to simplify the problem for the case of zero communication costs. While the zero-communication case is NP-hard for POT, it is easily solvable for POTP (a symmetric schedule is optimal). However, when communication costs are non-zero, POTP has an NP-hard problem embedded in it and falls in the class of non-linear, non-convex continuous optimization problems. We investigated two classes of schedules: balanced and symmetric. This led to a characterization of optimal schedules and several results on local minimization. We also showed that trees of size 2 may be optimally scheduled by a simple rule.

The overall contribution of our thesis is the development of models and algorithms for parallel query optimization that account for the benefit as well as the cost of parallel execution. We have used a formal approach in addition to experimentation on real systems and simulations. Our models capture opportunities for parallelism and obstacles to speedup that are likely to be applicable beyond database query processing to parallel computing applications such as N-body simulations [Her88, Kat89, Sal90, Sin93] in scientific computing and radiosity computations [M.F85, P. 91] in graphics.

6.2 Future Work

There are several open problems in the area of parallel query optimization. Some may be investigated within the models that we have proposed, other require extensions.

Integration of JOQR and Parallelization: An open issue is to devise and evaluate approaches for integrating the two phases of optimization so as to produce globally optimal plans. An interesting approach is to produce a set of plans as the output of the JOQR phase, parallelize each of them and take the best. Interesting questions are the criteria for choosing the set of plans, the size of the set, and an analysis of how close we get to the optimal plan.

Space-Time Trade-off: Scheduling problems may be characterized along two dimensions: the *machine* model and the *task* model. The machine model represents resources such as processors, disks, memory and the network. The task model consists of operator tree and the degrees of freedom that the scheduler is allowed (i.e. the use of partitioned, pipelined and independent parallelism).

One challenge is to incorporate space-time tradeoffs in the task model. It is well known that additional memory can be exploited to reduce the I/O and CPU cost of operations such as sorting. In a parallel machine, more memory is obtained by spreading computation over a larger number of processors – thus I/O and CPU can be traded for memory and communication. It is challenging to devise models and algorithms that minimize response time subject to limits on maximum memory usage while taking this trade-off into account.

Heterogeneous Architectures: It is standard for work in parallel query optimization to assume all nodes of a parallel machine to be identical. However, heterogeneity arises for several reasons. One often touted advantage of parallel machines is the ability to incrementally add components (processors, disks). It should be noted that by the time more computing power is needed, newer and faster components are likely to be available. A more general scenario for heterogeneity is the existence of a large number of diverse machines in most offices. Many of these machines are under-utilized, especially at night. Commodity interconnects such as Myrinet, FDDI or an ATM switch may be used to turn idle machine cycles into a useful parallel machine.

Distributed information systems may also be enabled by the ubiquity of WANs such as the Internet. At one end of the spectrum, when there is strong central control, these problems may be modeled by considering the system to be a heterogeneous parallel system. At the other end, decentralized resources management poses extremely challenging problems [SDK+94]. Further, these new environments may require new optimization objectives such as minimizing monetary cost to the end-user given response time constraints, or minimizing response time given a fixed budget.

Dynamic/Pre-emptive Optimization: The machine resources available for executing a query may change while the query is in execution. For example, another query may complete and release resources. This motivates the need for dynamic revision [BFV96] of scheduling decisions.

We observe that the additional freedom to revise scheduling decisions gave two advantages in classical scheduling problems such as multi-processor scheduling. Firstly, pre-emptive schedule provide better response times than non-preemptive schedules. Secondly, the algorithmic problems get simplified.

It can be costly to pre-empt a query that uses a large number of resources on a parallel machine. Any pre-emptive scheme must account for the trade-off between the cost and benefit of pre-emption.

Optimization decisions other than scheduling may also benefit from revision at execution time [Roy91, GW89]. Join ordering is sensitive to estimates of intermediate result sizes. It is well known that such estimates may have large errors and better information may be available at execution time.

Data Placement and Precedence Constraints: Data placement constrains the allocation of scan operators to specific processors. While this aspect can be easily incorporated into some of the algorithms such as *Greedy-Pairing*, we have not explored the issue in depth. We have also not developed scheduling algorithms that account for precedence constraints. While there is substantial work on precedence constraints in scheduling theory, the challenge is to account for the cost of communication. Since edges in operator trees represent the flow of data, a precedence constraint implies materialization of a set of tuples. Transferring such a set incurs substantial communication cost.

Cost Models: It is desirable to let users decide whether the cost of running a query is worth the benefit from the query result. This requires the ability to accurately predict query execution time. While this is a challenging problem even for sequential machines, factors such as data skew [WDJ91, DNSS92] pose additional challenges for parallel machines. More work is needed to develop and validate accurate cost models.

Database systems are increasingly deployed in interactive systems where it is important to minimize the time to produce the first screen-full of tuples of the query result rather than the time to complete the query. This new optimization objective poses fresh challenges.

References

[AHY83]   P.M.G. Apers, A.R. Hevner, and S.B. Yao. Optimization Algorithms for Distributed Queries. *IEEE Transaction on Software Engineering*, 9(1), 1983.

[ASU79]   A.V. Aho, Y. Sagiv, and J.D. Ullman. Efficient Optimization of a Class of Relational Expressions. *Transactions on Database Systems*, 4(4):435–454, 1979.

[AU79]   A.V. Aho and J.D. Ullman. Universality of Data Retrieval Languages. In *Principles of Programming Languages*, 1979.

[BB90]   K.P Belkhale and P. Banerjee. Approximate Algorithms for the Partitionable Independent Task Scheduling Problem. In *International Conference on Parallel Processing*, pages I–72 – I–75, 1990.

[BBT88]   B.Ball, W. Bartlett, and S. Thompson. Tandem's Approach to Fault Tolerance. *Tandem Systems Review*, 4(1), February 1988. Part Number 11078.

[BC81]   P. A. Bernstein and D.W. Chiu. Using Semi-Joins to Solve Relational Queries. *Journal of the ACM*, 28(1):25–40, January 1981.

[BCC+90] H. Boral, L. Clay, G. Copeland, S. Danforth, M. Franklin, B. Hart, M. Smith, and P. Valduriez. Prototyping Bubba, A Highly Parallel Database System. *IEEE Transactions on Knowledge and Data Engineering*, 2(1), March 1990.

[BE77]   M. W. Blasgen and K. P. Eswaran. Storage and Access in Relation Databases. *IBM Systems Journal*, 16(4):363–377, 1977.

[Bel57]   R.E. Bellman. *Dynamic Programming*. Princeton University Press, 1957.

[BFG+95] C.K. Baru, G. Fecteau, A. Goyal, H. Hsiao, A. Jhingran, S. Padmanabhan, G.P. Copeland, and W.G. Wilson. DB2 Parallel Edition. *IBM Systems Journal*, 34(2):292–322, 1995.

[BFV96]   L. Bouganim, D. Florescu, and P. Valduriez. Dynamic Load Balancing in Hierarchical Parallel Database Systems. In *Proceedings of the Twenty Second International Conference on Very Large Data Bases*, September 1996.

[BGW+81] P.A. Bernstein, N. Goodman, E. Wong, C.L. Reeve, and J.B. Rothnie. Query Processing in a System for Distributed Databases (SDD-1). *Transactions on Database Systems*, 6(4):602–625, December 1981.

[BHH78]   G. E. P. Box, W. G. Hunter, and J. S. Hunter. *Statistics for Experimenters*. John Wiley and Sons, 1978.

[BMV91]   B. Bergsten, M.Couprie, , and P. Valduriez. Prototyping DBS3, a Shared-Memory Parallel Database System. In *First International Conference on Parallel and Distributed Information Systems*, Miami Beach, Florida, December 1991.

[CABK88]   G. Copeland, W. Alexander, E. Boughter, and T. Keller. Data Place-ment in Bubba. In *Proceedings of ACM-SIGMOD International Conference on Management of Data*, 1988.

[CAE⁺76]   D. D. Chamberlin, M. M. Astrahan, K. P. Eswaran, P. P. Griffiths, R. A. Lorie,. J. W. Mehl, P. Reisner, and B. W. Wade. SEQUEL2: A Unified Approach to Data Definition, Manipulation, and Control. *IBM Journal of Research and Development*, 20(6):560–575, November 1976.

[CGK90]   D. Chimenti, R. Gamboa, and R. Krishnamurthy. Abstract machine for LDL. In *Proceedings of the Extending Database Technology Conference*, 1990.

[Cha88]   A. K. Chandra. Theory of Database Queries. In *Principles of Database Systems*, 1988.

[CHM95]   C. Chekuri, W. Hasan, and R. Motwani. Scheduling Problems in Parallel Query Optimization. In *Proceedings of the Fourteenth ACM SIGACT-SIGMOD-SIGART Symposium on Principles of Database Systems*, 1995.

[Chr84]   S. Christodoulakis. Implications of Certain Assumptions in Database Performance Evaluation. *Transactions on Database Systems*, 9(2):163–186, June 1984.

[CK92]   F. Carino and P. Kostamaa. Exegesis of DBC/1012 and P-90 - Industrial Supercomputer Database Machines. In *Parallel Architectures and Languages Europe*, Paris, France, June 1992.

[CKP⁺93]   David Culler, Richard Karp, David Patterson, Abhijit Sahay, Klaus Erik Schauser, Eunice Santos, Ramesh Subramonian, and Thorsten von Eicken. LogP: Towards a Realistic Model of Parallel Computation. In *Proceedings of the Fourth ACM SIGPLAN Symposium on Principles and Practice of Parallel Programming*, May 1993.

[CLYY92]   M-S Chen, M-L Lo, P.S. Yu, and H.C. Young. Using Segmented Right-Deep Trees for the Execution of Pipelined Hash Joins. In *Proceedings of the Eighteenth International Conference on Very Large Data Bases*, pages 15–26, June 1992.

[CM77]   A. K. Chandra and P. M. Merlin. Optimal Implementation of Conjunctive Queries in Relational Databases. In *Proceedings of the Ninth Annual ACM Symposium on Theory of Computing*, pages 77–99, 1977.

[CNW83]   S. Ceri, S. B. Navathe, and G. Wiederhold. Distribution Design of Logical Database Schemas. *IEEE Transactions on Software Engineering*, 9(4):487–563, July 1983.

[Cod70]   E. F. Codd. A Relational Model of Data for Large Shared Data Banks. *Communications of the ACM*, 13(6):377–387, June 1970.

[CP84]   S. Ceri. and G. Pelagatti. *Distributed Database Design: Principles and Systems*. McGraw-Hill, 1984.

[CR91]   S. Chopra and M.R. Rao. On the Multiway Cut Polyhedron. *Networks*, 21:51–89, 1991.

[CS94]   S. Chaudhuri and K. Shim. Including group-by in query optimization. In *Proceedings of the Twentieth International Conference on Very Large Data Bases*, Santiago, Chile, September 1994.

[Dav78]   O. L. Davies, editor. *The Design and Analysis of Industrial Experiments*. Longman Group Limited, 2nd edition, 1978.

[Day87]   U. Dayal. Of Nests and Trees: A Unified Approach to Processing Queries That Contain Nested Subqueries, Aggregates, and Quantifiers. In *Proceedings of the Thirteenth International Conference on Very Large Data Bases*, Brighton, England, 1987.

[DG90]   D. J. DeWitt and J. Gray. Parallel Database Systems: The Future
            of Database Processing or a Passing Fad? *ACM-SIGMOD Record*,
            19(4):104–112, December 1990.

[DG92]   D. J. DeWitt and J. Gray. Parallel Database Systems: The Future of
            High Performance Database Systems. *Communications of the ACM*,
            35(6):85–98, June 1992.

[DGG+86]   D. DeWitt, R. Gerber, G. Graefe, M. Heytens, K. Kumar, and M. Mu-
            ralikrishna. GAMMA: A High Performance Dataflow Database Ma-
            chine. In *Proceedings of the Twelfth International Conference on Very
            Large Data Bases*, August 1986.

[DGS+90]   D.J. DeWitt, S. Ghandeharizadeh, D. Schneider, A. Bricker, H.-I.
            Hsiao, and R. Rasmussen. The Gamma database machine project.
            IEEE Transactions on Knowledge and Data Engineering, 2(1), March
            1990.

[DJP+92]   E. Dahlhaus, D. S. Johnson, C. H. Papadimitriou, P. D. Seymour,
            and M. Yannakakis. Complexity of Multiway Cuts. In *Proceedings of
            the 24th Annual ACM Symposium on the Theory of Computing*, pages
            241–251, 1992.

[DNSS92]   D. DeWitt, J. Naughton, D. Schneider, and S. Seshadri. Practical
            Skew Handling in Parallel Joins. In *Proceedings of the Eighteenth In-
            ternational Conference on Very Large Data Bases*, Vancouver, British
            Columbia, Canada, August 1992.

[DV92]   S. Danforth and P. Valduriez. A FAD for Data-Intensive Applications.
            IEEE Transactions on Knowledge and Data Engineering, 4(1), March
            1992.

[DW83]   S. Dowdy and S. Wearden. *Statistics for Research.* John Wiley and
            Sons, 1983.

[EAC86]   K. Ekanadham, Arvind, and D.E. Culler. The Price of Parallelism.
            Technical report, M.I.T, 1986. Computer Science Department TR 86-
            731.

[EGH95]   S. Englert, R. Glasstone, and W. Hasan. Parallelism and its Price: A
            Case Study of NonStop SQL/MP. *Sigmod Record*, 24(4), December
            1995.

[EGKS89]   S. Englert, J. Gray, T. Kocher, and P. Stah. A Benchmark of Non-
            Stop SQL Release 2 Demonstrating Near-Linear Speedup and Scaleup
            on Large Databases. Technical report, Tandem Computers, May 1989.
            Technical Report 89.4, Tandem Part No. 27469.

[ES80]   R. Epstein and M. Stonebraker. Analysis of Distributed Database Pro-
            cessing Strategies. In *Proceedings of the Fifth International Conference
            on Very Large Data Bases*, pages 92–101, October 1980.

[ES92]   P.L. Erdos and L.A. Szekely. Evolutionary Trees: An Integer Multi-
            commodity Max-Flow-Min-Cut Theorem. *Advances in Applied Math-
            ematics*, 13:375–389, 1992.

[ES94]   P.L. Erdos and L.A. Szekely. On Weighted Multiway Cuts in Trees.
            Mathematical Programming, 65:93–105, 1994.

[Eve79]   S. Even. *Graph Algorithms.* Computer Science Press, 1979.

[GHK92]   S. Ganguly, W. Hasan, and R. Krishnamurthy. Query Optimization
            for Parallel Execution. In *Proceedings of ACM-SIGMOD International
            Conference on Management of Data*, pages 9–18, June 1992.

[GHQ95]   A. Gupta, V. Harinarayan, and D. Quass. Aggregate-query processing
            in data warehousing environments. In *Proceedings of the Twenty First
            International Conference on Very Large Data Bases*, Zurich, Switzer-
            land, September 1995.

[GJ79]   M.R. Garey and D.S. Johnson. *Computers and Intractability*. W.H. Freeman and Company, 1979.

[GLLK79]   R.L Graham, E.L. Lawler, J.K. Lenstra, and A.H.G Rinnooy Kan. Optimization and Approximation in Deterministic Sequencing and Scheduling: A Survey. *Annals of Discrete Mathematics*, 5:287–326, 1979.

[GM78]   H. Gallaire and J. Minker, editors. *Logic and Databases*. Plenum Press, New York, 1978.

[GMW81]   P.E. Gill, W. Murray, and M.H. Wright. *Practical Optimization*. Academic Press, 1981.

[GR93]   J. Gray and A. Reuter. *Transaction Processing: Concepts and Techniques*. Morgan Kaufmann, 1993.

[Gra69]   R.L. Graham. Bounds on Multiprocessing Timing Anomalies. *SIAM Journal of Applied Mathematics*, 17(2):416–429, March 1969.

[Gra88]   J. Gray. The Cost of Messages. In *Proceedings of the Seventh ACM Symposium on Principles of Distributed Computing*, pages 1–7, Toronto, Ontario, Canada, August 1988.

[Gra90]   G. Graefe. Encapsulation of Parallelism in the Volcano Query Processing System. In *Proceedings of ACM-SIGMOD International Conference on Management of Data*, May 1990.

[Gra91]   J. Gray. *The Benchmark Handbook for Database and Transaction Processing Systems*. Morgan Kaufmann Publishers, Inc., 1991.

[GW87]   R.A. Ganski and H.K.T Wong. Optimization of Nested SQL Queries Revisited. In *Proceedings of ACM-SIGMOD International Conference on Management of Data*, 1987.

[GW89]   G. Graefe and K. Ward. Dynamic Query Optimization Plans. In *Proceedings of ACM-SIGMOD International Conference on Management of Data*, May 1989.

[Had74]   F.O. Hadlock. Minimum Spanning Forests of Bounded Trees. In *Proceedings of the 5th Southeastern Conference on Combinatorics, Graph Theory and Computing*, pages 449–460. Utilitas Mathematica Publishing, Winnipeg, 1974.

[Hal76]   P.A.V. Hall. Optimization of a Single Relational Expression in a Relational Data Base. *IBM Journal of Research and Development*, 20(3):244–257, May 1976.

[HDV88]   B. Hart, S. Danforth, and P. Valduriez. Parallelizing FAD, A Database Programming Language. In *International Symposium on Databases in Parallel and Distributed Systems*, Austin, Texas, December 1988.

[Her88]   L. Hernquist. Hierarchical N-body Methods. *Computer Physics Communications*, 48:107–115, 1988.

[HFLP89]   L.M. Haas, J.C. Freytag, G.M. Lohman, and H. Pirahesh. Extensible Query Processing in Starburst. In *Proceedings of ACM-SIGMOD International Conference on Management of Data*, June 1989.

[HFV96]   W. Hasan, D. Florescu, and P. Valduriez. Open Issues in Parallel Query Optimization. *Sigmod Record*, 25(3), September 1996.

[HJT94]   F. Ho, R. Jain, and J. Troisi. An Overview of NonStop SQL/MP. *Tandem Systems Review*, pages 6–17, July 1994.

[HLY93]   K.A. Hua, Y. Lo, and H.C. Young. Including the Load Balancing Issue in The Optimization of Multi-way Join Queries for Shared-Nothing Database Computer. In *Second International Conference on Parallel and Distributed Information Systems*, San Diego, California, January 1993.

[HM93]   A. Hameurlain and F. Morvan. A parallel scheduling method for effi-
            cient query processing. In *Proceedings of the 22nd International Con-
            ference on Parallel Processing*, St. Charles, Illinois, August 1993.

[HM94a]   A. Hameurlain and F. Morvan. Scheduling and parallelism for ex-
            tended sql query optimization. In *Proceedings of the 7th Intl. Conf.
            on Parallel and Distributed Computing Systems*, Las Vegas, Nevada,
            October 1994.

[HM94b]   W. Hasan and R. Motwani. Optimization Algorithms for Exploiting
            the Parallelism-Communication Tradeoff in Pipelined Parallelism. In
            *Proceedings of the Twentieth International Conference on Very Large
            Data Bases*, pages 36–47, Santiago, Chile, September 1994.

[HM95]   W. Hasan and R. Motwani. Coloring Away Communication in Parallel
            Query Optimization. In *Proceedings of the Twenty First International
            Conference on Very Large Data Bases*, Zurich, Switzerland, September
            1995.

[Hon92a]   W. Hong. Exploiting Inter-Operation Parallelism in XPRS. In *Pro-
            ceedings of ACM-SIGMOD International Conference on Management
            of Data*, June 1992.

[Hon92b]   W. Hong. *Parallel Query Processing Using Shared Memory Multipro-
            cessors and Disk Arrays*. PhD thesis, University of California, Berke-
            ley, August 1992.

[HS91]   W. Hong and M. Stonebraker. Optimization of Parallel Query Exe-
            cution Plans in XPRS. In *Proceedings of the First International Con-
            ference on Parallel and Distributed Information Systems*, December
            1991.

[Hu61]   T.C. Hu. Parallel Sequencing and Assembly Line Problems. *Operations
            Research*, 9(6):841–848, November 1961.

[IK84]   T. Ibaraki and T. Kameda. Optimal Nesting for Computing N-
            relational Joins. *Transactions on Database Systems*, 9(3):482–502, Oc-
            tober 1984.

[Inf95]   Informix. INFORMIX-OnLine Extended Parallel Server for Loosely
            Coupled Cluster and Massively Parallel Processing Architectures, July
            1995. HTML document http://www.informix.com.

[JK84]   M. Jarke and J. Koch. Query Optimization in Database Systems.
            ACM Computing Surveys, 16(2):111–152, June 1984.

[Kat89]   J. Katznelson. Computational Structure of the N-body problem. *SIAM
            Journal of Scientific and Statistical Computing*, 10(4):787–815, 1989.

[Ker71]   B. W. Kernighan. Optimal Sequential Partitions of Graphs. *Journal
            of the ACM*, 18(1):34–40, January 1971.

[KGV83]   S. Kirkpatrick, C. D. Gelatt, and M. P. Vecchi. Optimization by Sim-
            ulated Annealing. *Science*, 220(4598):671–680, May 1983.

[KHA86]   Y. Kiyoki, R. Hasegawa, and M. Amamiya. A stream-oriented parallel
            processing scheme for relational database operations. In *Proceedings
            of International Conf. on Parallel Processing*, 1986.

[Kim82]   W. Kim. On Optimizing an SQL-like Nested Query. *Transactions on
            Database Systems*, 7(3), September 1982.

[Kin81]   J. J. King. *Query Optimization by Semantic Reasoning*. PhD thesis,
            Stanford University, 1981. Stanford CS Report STAN-CS-81-857.

[Knu73]   D. E. Knuth. *The Art of Computer Programming, Vol 1: Fundamental
            Algorithms*. Addison-Wesley, 2nd edition, 1973.

[KRB85]   W. Kim, D. S. Reiner, and D. S. Batory, editors. *Query Processing in
            Database Systems*. Springer-Verlag, 1985.

[KV87]   S. Khoshafian and P. Valduriez. Parallel Execution Strategies for Declustered Databases. In *Proceedings of the Fifth International Workshop on Database Machines*, Karuizawa, Japan, October 1987.

[KV89]   S. Khoshafian and P. Valduriez. A Parallel Container Model for Data Intensive Applications. In *Proceedings of the Sixth International Workshop on Database Machines*, Deauville, France, June 1989.

[LCRY93]   M-L. Lo, M-S. Chen, C.V. Ravishankar, and P.S. Yu. On Optimal Processor Allocation to Support Pipelined Hash Joins. In *Proceedings of ACM-SIGMOD International Conference on Management of Data*, pages 69–78, June 1993.

[LMH⁺85]   G. Lohman, C. Mohan, L. Haas, D. Daniels, B. Lindsay, P. Selinger, and P. Wilms. Query Processing in R*. In W. Kim, D. Reiner, and D. S. Batory, editors, *Query Processing in Database Systems*. Springer Verlag, 1985.

[LMS94]   A. Y. Levy, I. S. Mumick, and Y. Sagiv. Query optimization by predicate move-around. In *Proceedings of the Twentieth International Conference on Very Large Data Bases*, Santiago, Chile, September 1994.

[LST91]   H. Lu, M-C. Shan, and K-L. Tan. Optimization of Multi-Way Join Queries for Parallel Execution. In *Proceedings of the Seventeenth International Conference on Very Large Data Bases*, Barcelona, Spain, September 1991.

[Lue89]   D.G. Luenberger. *Linear and Nonlinear Optimization*. Addison-Wesley Publishing Company, second edition, 1989.

[Luk74]   J. A. Lukes. Efficient Algorithm for the Partitioning of Trees. *IBM Journal of Research and Development*, 18(3):217–224, May 1974.

[LVZ93]   R.S.G Lanzelotte, P. Valduriez, and M. Zait. On the Effectiveness of Optimization Search Strategies for Parallel Execution Spaces. In *Proceedings of the Nineteenth International Conference on Very Large Data Bases*, Dublin, Ireland, 1993.

[MC70]   R.R. Muntz and E.G. Coffman. Preemptive Scheduling of Real-Time Tasks on Multiprocessor Systems. *Journal of the ACM*, 17(2):324–338, April 1970.

[McN59]   R. McNaughton. Scheduling with Deadlines and Loss Functions. *Management Science*, 6(1):1–12, October 1959.

[M.F85]   M.F.Cohen and D.P.Greenberg. The Hemi-cube: A Radiosity Solution for Complex Environments. In *Proceedings of SIGGRAPH*, 1985.

[ML86]   L. F. Mackert and G. M. Lohman. R* Optimizer Validation and Performance Evaluation for Local Queries. Technical report, IBM Research Division, January 1986. IBM Research Report RJ 4989.

[Mot92]   R. Motwani. *Lecture Notes on Approximation Algorithms (Volume I)*. Report No. STAN-CS-92-1435, Department of Computer Science, Stanford University, June 1992.

[MPTW94]   C. Mohan, H. Pirahesh, W.G. Tang, and Y. Wang. Parallelism in Relational Database Management Systems. *IBM Systems Journal*, 33(2), 1994.

[Ora95]   Oracle. Oracle Parallel Server, 1995. HTML document from http://www.oracle.com.

[OV91]   M.T. Ozsu and P. Valduriez. *Principles of Distributed Database Systems*. Prentice-Hall, 1991.

[P. 91]   P. Hanrahan and D. Satzman and L. Aupperle. A Rapid Hierarchical Radiosity Algorithm. In *Proceedings of SIGGRAPH*, 1991.

[PHH92]   H. Pirahesh, J.M. Hellerstein, and W. Hasan. Extensible/Rule Based Query Rewrite Optimization in Starburst. In *Proceedings of ACM-SIGMOD International Conference on Management of Data*, June 1992.

[PLH95]   H. Pirahesh, C. Leung, and W. Hasan. Rule Engine for Query Transformation in Starburst and DB2/CS DBMS. Technical report, IBM Almaden Research Center, San Jose, CA, March 1995. IBM Internal Research Report RJ 9943(87902).

[PMC+90]   H. Pirahesh, C. Mohan, J. Cheung, T.S. Liu, and P. Selinger. Parallelism in Relational Data Base Systems: Architectural Issues and Design Approaches. In *Second International Symposium on Databases in Parallel and Distributed Systems*, Dublin, Ireland, 1990.

[PS82]   C. H. Papadimitriou and K. Steiglitz. *Combinatorial Optimization: Algorithms and Complexity*. Prentice-Hall, 1982.

[PU87]   C.H. Papadimitriou and J.D. Ullman. A Communication-Time Tradeoff. *SIAM Journal of Computing*, 16(4):639–646, August 1987.

[PY88]   C.H. Papadimitriou and M. Yannakakis. Towards an Architecture-Independent Analysis of Parallel Algorithms. In *Symposium on Theory of Computing*, pages 510–513, 1988.

[Roy91]   S. Roy. *Adaptive Methods in Parallel Databases*. PhD thesis, Stanford University, 1991. Stanford CS Report STAN-CS-91-1397.

[SAB+89]   M. Smith, W. Alexander, H. Boral, G. Copeland, T. Keller, H Schwetman, and C-R Young. An Experiment on Response Time Scalability in Bubba. In *Proceedings of the Sixth International Workshop on Database Machines*, Deauville, France, June 1989.

[SAC+79]   P. Selinger, M. M. Astrahan, D. D. Chamberlin, R. A. Lorie, and T. G. Price. Access Path Selection in a Relational Database Management System. In *Proceedings of ACM-SIGMOD International Conference on Management of Data*, 1979.

[Sal90]   J.K. Salmon. *Parallel Hierarchical N-Body Methods*. PhD thesis, California Institute of Technology, December 1990.

[Sch90]   D. A. Schneider. *Complex Query Processing in Multiprocessor Database Machines*. PhD thesis, University of Wisconsin—Madison, September 1990. Computer Sciences Technical Report 965.

[SD89]   D. A. Schneider and D. J. DeWitt. A performance evaluation of four parallel join algorithms in a shared-nothing multiprocessor environment. In *ACM SIGMOD*, Portland, Oregon, June 1989.

[SD90]   D.A. Schneider and D.J. DeWitt. Tradeoffs in Processing Complex Join Queries via Hashing in Multiprocessor Database Machines. In *Proceedings of the Sixteenth International Conference on Very Large Data Bases*, Brisbane, Australia, 1990.

[SDK+94]   M. Stonebraker, R. Devine, M. Kornacker, W. Litwin, A. Pfeffer, A. Sah, and C. Staelin. An Economic Paradigm for Query Processing and Data Migration in Mariposa. In *Third International Conference on Parallel and Distributed Information Systems*, Austin, Texas, September 1994.

[SE93]   J. Srivastava and G. Elsesser. Optimizing Multi-Join Queries in Parallel Relational Databases. In *Second International Conference on Parallel and Distributed Information Systems*, San Diego, California, January 1993.

[Sin93]   J. P. Singh. *Parallel Hierarchical N-Body Methods and their Implications for Multiprocessors*. PhD thesis, Stanford University, March 1993. Stanford CSL Report CSL-TR-93-565.

[SP92]   P. Valduriez S. Parker, E. Simon. SVP, a Data Model Capturing
           Sets, Streams and Parallelism. In *Proceedings of the Eighteenth In-
           ternational Conference on Very Large Data Bases*, Vancouver, British
           Columbia, Canada, August 1992.

[SW85]   D. Sacca and G. Wiederhold. Database Partitioning in a Cluster of
           Processors. *Transactions on Database Systems*, 10(1):29–56, March
           1985.

[SW91]   D. Shasha and T.L. Wang. Optimizing Equijoin Queries in Distributed
           Databases where Relations are Hash Partitioned. *Transactions on
           Database Systems*, 16(2):279–308, June 1991.

[Swa89]   A. Swami. *Optimization of Large Join Queries*. PhD thesis, Stanford
           University, 1989. Stanford CS Report STAN-CS-89-1262.

[SY91]   A. Swami and H.C. Young. Online Algorithms for Handling Skew in
           Parallel Joins. Technical report, IBM Research Division, September
           1991. IBM Research Report RJ 8363(76086).

[SYG92]   A. Swami, H.C. Young, and A. Gupta. Algorithms for Handling Skew
           in Parallel Task Scheduling. *Journal of Parallel and Distributed Com-
           puting*, 16:363–377, 1992.

[SYT93]   E. J. Shekita, H.C. Young, and K-L Tan. Multi-Join Optimization
           for Symmetric Multiprocessors. In *Proceedings of the Nineteenth In-
           ternational Conference on Very Large Data Bases*, Dublin, Ireland,
           1993.

[Tan]   Tandem. Cyclone/R Message System Performance. Technical report,
           Tandem Computers.

[Tan94]   Tandem. NonStop SQL/MP Reference Manual, December 1994. Tan-
           dem Part Number 100149, Release ID D30.00.

[Tan95]   Tandem. Query Processing Using NonStop SQL/MP, 1995. HTML
           document from http://www.tandem.com.

[TWPY92]   J. Turek, J.L. Wolf, K.R. Pattipati, and P.S. Yu. Scheduling Paral-
           lelizable Tasks: Putting it All on the Shelf. In *Proceedings of the ACM
           Sigmetrics Conference on Measurement and Modeling of Computer
           Systems*, June 1992.

[Ull75]   J.D. Ullman. NP-Complete Scheduling Problems. *JCSS*, 10:384–393,
           1975.

[Ull89]   J. D. Ullman. *Principles of Database and Knowledge-base Systems*.
           Computer Science Press, 1989.

[Val93]   P. Valduriez. Parallel Database Systems: Open Problems and New
           Issues. *Distributed and Parallel Databases: An International Journal*,
           1(2):137–165, April 1993.

[vB89]   Gunter von Bulltzingsloewen. Optimizing SQL Queries for Parallel
           Execution. *ACM-SIGMOD Record*, 18(4):17–22, December 1989.

[VD89]   P. Valduriez and S. Danforth. Query Optimization in Database Pro-
           gramming Languages. In *Proceedings of International Conference on
           Deductive Object-Oriented Databases*, Kyoto, Japan, December 1989.

[VG84]   P. Valduriez and G. Gardarin. Join and Semijoin Algorithms for a
           Multiprocessor Database Machine. *Transactions on Database Systems*,
           9(1):133–161, March 1984.

[WDJ91]   C.B. Walton, A.G. Dale, and R.M. Jenevein. A Taxonomy and Perfor-
           mance Model of Data Skew Effects in Parallel Joins. In *Proceedings of
           the Seventeenth International Conference on Very Large Data Bases*,
           Barcelona, Spain, September 1991.

[WFA92]   A.N. Wilschut, J. Flokstra, and P.M. Apers. Parallelism in a main-
           memory dbms: The performance of prisma/db. In *Proceedings of the*

	Eighteenth International Conference on Very Large Data Bases, Vancouver, British Columbia, Canada, August 1992.
[Wie81]	G. Wiederhold. Binding in Information Processing. Technical report, Stanford University, May 1981. Computer Science Report STAN-CS-81-851.
[Wie86]	G. Wiederhold. Views, Objects and Databases. *IEEE Computer*, pages 37–44, December 1986.
[Wie87]	G. Wiederhold. *File Organization for Database Design*. McGraw-Hill, 1987.
[Wol88]	S. Wolfram. *Mathematica: A System for Doing Mathematics by Computer*. Addison-Wesley Publishing Company, 1988.
[WY76]	E. Wong and K. Youseffi. Decomposition - A Strategy for Query Processing. *Transactions on Database Systems*, 1(3):223–241, September 1976.
[X3H92]	X3H2. Information technology - database language sql, July 1992. Also available as International Standards Organization document ISO/IEC:9075:1992.
[YC84]	C.T. Yu and C.C. Chang. Distributed Query Processing. *ACM Computing Surveys*, 16(4), December 1984.
[YL94]	W. P. Yan and P. A. Larson. Performing Group-By before Join. In *Proceedings of IEEE Data Engineering Conference*, Houston, February 1994.
[YL95]	W. P. Yan and P. A. Larson. Eager Aggregation and Lazy Aggregation. In *Proceedings of the Twenty First International Conference on Very Large Data Bases*, Zurich, Switzerland, September 1995.
[ZG90]	H. Zeller and J. Gray. Hash Join Algorithms in a Multiuser Environment. In *Proceedings of the Sixteenth International Conference on Very Large Data Bases*, Brisbane, Australia, 1990.
[ZZBS93]	M. Ziane, M. Zait, and P. Borla-Salamet. Parallel Query Processing in DBS3. In *Second International Conference on Parallel and Distributed Information Systems*, San Diego, California, January 1993.

Index

Access methods 39, 47, 56
Aggregation 2, 17, 22, 24, 25, 30, 31, 37
Attribute insensitive *see* Operator
Attribute sensitive *see* Operator
Available parallelism 1–3, 7, 10, 33, 115

BalancedCuts algorithm 72, 73, 78
BoundedCuts algorithm 79, 84, 85, 88, 89, 91–94, 118
Bubba project 10

Color pattern 50, 51
ColorSplit algorithm 39, 46, 47, 52, 54
Communication
– cost 2, 3, 5, 7, 8, 10, 13–14, 21, 23, 31, 33, 35, 36, 38, 47, 48, 50, 59, 62, 63, 66, 68, 73, 76, 78, 80, 82–85, 95, 102, 108–112, 115, 116, 118, 120
– local 14, 20, 22, 24–26, 30
– message based 16
– remote 14, 20, 24–26, 33
– repartitioned 26, 38, 48
– shared-memory 34
Compound attributes 47, 48
Constraint
– concave 98
– convex 98
– data placement 3, 115, 118, 120
– input-output 50–52, 117
– linear 98
– non-linear 98
– parallel 3, 6–7, 60
– pipelining 60, 96
– precedence 3, 6–7, 120
– timing 3–6, 115
Context switch 68, 94, 118
Continuous optimization 95, 118
Convex programming 98
Cost model 38, 50, 54, 55, 60

Data placement *see* Constraint
DBS3 project 10
Disk process *see* Process
DLC algorithm 39, 43, 44
DP2 *see* Disk process
Duplicate elimination 2

Edge
– collapse 62
– cut 62
– worthless 62–66, 74
Eigenvalue 98, 106, 108
ESP *see* Executor server process
Except operator 37
Executor server process *see* Process
ExtendedColorSplit algorithm 53, 56

Fragment and replicate *see* Parallelism

Gamma project 10, 38
Gantt chart 60, 97
Good scheduler 38
GreedyChase algorithm 62, 65, 66, 73, 78
GreedyPairing algorithm 78, 79, 94, 118
Grouping operator 2, 35, 37, 47, 49, 116
– hash 17, 22, 30, 49
– parallelization 17
– sort 17, 22, 30

Hessian 98, 105
Hybrid algorithm 68, 78, 89, 91–94, 117, 118
Hybrid-hash join *see* Join

Independent parallelism *see* Parallelism
Index *see* Physical property, 47

Intersect operator   3, 37, 45

Jacobian matrix   105
JO algorithm   55
Join
– hybrid-hash   18–20, 22
– nested-loops   18
– parallelization   17–18
– sort-merge   22, 50
Join operator   3, 22, 47, 116
Join ordering   4, 35, 53–57, 117
Join ordering algorithm   see JO
Join predicate   47
Join tree cost   54, 55
JOP algorithm   56
JOQR phase   4, 35, 115–118

Knapsack   81

Lagrangian function   104, 105
Linear programming   98
Local minima   98–100, 103, 105, 110
– strong   101
– weak   101
LocalCuts algorithm   79, 82–84, 89,
   91–94, 118
Lower bound   65, 72, 90
LPT algorithm   62, 67

Message cost   see Communication
Minimal coloring   42–46
Modified LPT algorithm   66, 67, 78
Monotone tree   see Tree, kinds of
Mother node   see Node
Multiprocessor scheduling   60
Multiway cut   35, 39

Naive LPT algorithm   62
Near-optimal algorithm   59
Nested-loops join   see Join
Network topology   8
Node
– collapse   41
– color   38
– interior   50
– mother   42, 70
– split   40
– uncolored   44
Non-convex optimization   118
Non-linear optimization   118
NonStop SQL   5, 8, 13, 14, 17, 18, 23,
   30, 116

Operator

– attribute insensitive   36
– attribute sensitive   36, 48
– consumer   59
– partitionable   36
– producer   59
Operator tree   see Tree
Optimal schedule   8, 63, 67, 80, 84–86,
   89–92, 95, 99, 103, 111

Parallel constraint   see Constraint
Parallelism, forms of
– fragment and replicate   3, 18
– independent   2, 7, 10, 119
– inter-operator   17
– intra-operator   17
– partitioned   2–3, 7, 10, 119
– pipelined   2, 7, 10, 17, 119
Parallelization phase   4, 8, 10, 35, 115,
   117, 118
Partition and replicate   see Fragment
   and replicate
Partitioned parallelism   see Parallelism
Partitioning   36, 117
– horizontal   36, 47
– range   16
Partitioning function   48
Performance ratio   59, 62, 66, 67, 73,
   76–79, 81, 84, 88–92, 103, 117
Physical property   35, 48, 55
– index   35, 50, 117
– partitioning   50
– sort-order   35, 50, 117
Pipelined execution   7, 17
Pipelined operator tree   see Tree
Pipelined parallelism   see Parallelism
Precedence constraint   see Constraint
Process
– disk (DP2)   17, 19
– executor server process (ESP)   19,
   20, 33
– reuse   8, 13
– SQL executor   18, 31
Processor load   59, 95
Processor utilization   60, 96
Projected tree   see Tree
Projection operator   2, 37
Propagation delay   7

Quadratic programming   98
Query optimization
– distributed   9
– dynamic   119

– parallel   1
Query optimization, objectives
– first screen-full   120
– response time   1, 115
– response time and memory   119
– response time and money   119
– total work   115
Query tree   *see* Tree
Query tree coloring   38
Query tree cost   51, 54, 55

R* project   10
Range Partitioning   *see* Partitioning
Recoloring cost   51
Repeated colors   44
Response time   1, 60, 65, 96

Scan operator   25, 116
Scan parallelization   17, 19
Schedule   59, 95
– (B,p)-bounded   70
– balanced   8, 95, 99, 118
– connected   68, 78, 117
– equality   98
– interior   103
– pre-emptive   119
– symmetric   8, 38, 95, 103, 110, 118
SDD-1 project   10
Selection operator   2, 37
Shared-nothing architecture   14
Simplify algorithm   41, 46
Smoothness   98
Sort-merge join   *see* Join
Sort-order   *see* Physical property
SQL executor process   *see* Process
Starburst project   9
Startup cost   3, 13, 20, 33, 116
Statistics   51
Strategy   48
System R project   9, 54

Tree coloring   35, 116
Tree, kinds of
– join   10, 54
– left-deep   55
– monotone   63, 117
– narrow   90
– operator   5, 117
– path   62, 73
– pipelined operator   59
– query   5, 50
– right-deep   10
– segmented   10
– star   62, 73

– wide   90
– zig-zag   10
Tree, projection of   100
Two-phase optimization   4, 115, 118

Union operator   2, 37, 45

Volcano project   10

Worthless edge   *see* Edge
Worthless parallelism   62

XPRS project   10

Springer
and the
environment

At Springer we firmly believe that an international science publisher has a special obligation to the environment, and our corporate policies consistently reflect this conviction.
We also expect our business partners – paper mills, printers, packaging manufacturers, etc. – to commit themselves to using materials and production processes that do not harm the environment. The paper in this book is made from low- or no-chlorine pulp and is acid free, in conformance with international standards for paper permanency.

 Springer

Lecture Notes in Computer Science

For information about Vols. 1–1107

please contact your bookseller or Springer-Verlag

Vol. 1108: A. Díaz de Ilarraza Sánchez, I. Fernández de Castro (Eds.), Computer Aided Learning and Instruction in Science and Engineering. Proceedings, 1996. XIV, 480 pages. 1996.

Vol. 1109: N. Koblitz (Ed.), Advances in Cryptology – Crypto '96. Proceedings, 1996. XII, 417 pages. 1996.

Vol. 1110: O. Danvy, R. Glück, P. Thiemann (Eds.), Partial Evaluation. Proceedings, 1996. XII, 514 pages. 1996.

Vol. 1111: J.J. Alferes, L. Moniz Pereira, Reasoning with Logic Programming. XXI, 326 pages. 1996. (Subseries LNAI).

Vol. 1112: C. von der Malsburg, W. von Seelen, J.C. Vorbrüggen, B. Sendhoff (Eds.), Artificial Neural Networks – ICANN 96. Proceedings, 1996. XXV, 922 pages. 1996.

Vol. 1113: W. Penczek, A. Szałas (Eds.), Mathematical Foundations of Computer Science 1996. Proceedings, 1996. X, 592 pages. 1996.

Vol. 1114: N. Foo, R. Goebel (Eds.), PRICAI'96: Topics in Artificial Intelligence. Proceedings, 1996. XXI, 658 pages. 1996. (Subseries LNAI).

Vol. 1115: P.W. Eklund, G. Ellis, G. Mann (Eds.), Conceptual Structures: Knowledge Representation as Interlingua. Proceedings, 1996. XIII, 321 pages. 1996. (Subseries LNAI).

Vol. 1116: J. Hall (Ed.), Management of Telecommunication Systems and Services. XXI, 229 pages. 1996.

Vol. 1117: A. Ferreira, J. Rolim, Y. Saad, T. Yang (Eds.), Parallel Algorithms for Irregularly Structured Problems. Proceedings, 1996. IX, 358 pages. 1996.

Vol. 1118: E.C. Freuder (Ed.), Principles and Practice of Constraint Programming — CP 96. Proceedings, 1996. XIX, 574 pages. 1996.

Vol. 1119: U. Montanari, V. Sassone (Eds.), CONCUR '96: Concurrency Theory. Proceedings, 1996. XII, 751 pages. 1996.

Vol. 1120: M. Deza. R. Euler, I. Manoussakis (Eds.), Combinatorics and Computer Science. Proceedings, 1995. IX, 415 pages. 1996.

Vol. 1121: P. Perner, P. Wang, A. Rosenfeld (Eds.), Advances in Structural and Syntactical Pattern Recognition. Proceedings, 1996. X, 393 pages. 1996.

Vol. 1122: H. Cohen (Ed.), Algorithmic Number Theory. Proceedings, 1996. IX, 405 pages. 1996.

Vol. 1123: L. Bougé, P. Fraigniaud, A. Mignotte, Y. Robert (Eds.), Euro-Par'96. Parallel Processing. Proceedings, 1996, Vol. I. XXXIII, 842 pages. 1996.

Vol. 1124: L. Bougé, P. Fraigniaud, A. Mignotte, Y. Robert (Eds.), Euro-Par'96. Parallel Processing. Proceedings, 1996, Vol. II. XXXIII, 926 pages. 1996.

Vol. 1125: J. von Wright, J. Grundy, J. Harrison (Eds.), Theorem Proving in Higher Order Logics. Proceedings, 1996. VIII, 447 pages. 1996.

Vol. 1126: J.J. Alferes, L. Moniz Pereira, E. Orlowska (Eds.), Logics in Artificial Intelligence. Proceedings, 1996. IX, 417 pages. 1996. (Subseries LNAI).

Vol. 1127: L. Böszörményi (Ed.), Parallel Computation. Proceedings, 1996. XI, 235 pages. 1996.

Vol. 1128: J. Calmet, C. Limongelli (Eds.), Design and Implementation of Symbolic Computation Systems. Proceedings, 1996. IX, 356 pages. 1996.

Vol. 1129: J. Launchbury, E. Meijer, T. Sheard (Eds.), Advanced Functional Programming. Proceedings, 1996. VII, 238 pages. 1996.

Vol. 1130: M. Haveraaen, O. Owe, O.-J. Dahl (Eds.), Recent Trends in Data Type Specification. Proceedings, 1995. VIII, 551 pages. 1996.

Vol. 1131: K.H. Höhne, R. Kikinis (Eds.), Visualization in Biomedical Computing. Proceedings, 1996. XII, 610 pages. 1996.

Vol. 1132: G.-R. Perrin, A. Darte (Eds.), The Data Parallel Programming Model. XV, 284 pages. 1996.

Vol. 1133: J.-Y. Chouinard, P. Fortier, T.A. Gulliver (Eds.), Information Theory and Applications II. Proceedings, 1995. XII, 309 pages. 1996.

Vol. 1134: R. Wagner, H. Thoma (Eds.), Database and Expert Systems Applications. Proceedings, 1996. XV, 921 pages. 1996.

Vol. 1135: B. Jonsson, J. Parrow (Eds.), Formal Techniques in Real-Time and Fault-Tolerant Systems. Proceedings, 1996. X, 479 pages. 1996.

Vol. 1136: J. Diaz, M. Serna (Eds.), Algorithms – ESA '96. Proceedings, 1996. XII, 566 pages. 1996.

Vol. 1137: G. Görz, S. Hölldobler (Eds.), KI-96: Advances in Artificial Intelligence. Proceedings, 1996. XI, 387 pages. 1996. (Subseries LNAI).

Vol. 1138: J. Calmet, J.A. Campbell, J. Pfalzgraf (Eds.), Artificial Intelligence and Symbolic Mathematical Computation. Proceedings, 1996. VIII, 381 pages. 1996.

Vol. 1139: M. Hanus, M. Rogriguez-Artalejo (Eds.), Algebraic and Logic Programming. Proceedings, 1996. VIII, 345 pages. 1996.

Vol. 1140: H. Kuchen, S. Doaitse Swierstra (Eds.), Programming Languages: Implementations, Logics, and Programs. Proceedings, 1996. XI, 479 pages. 1996.

Vol. 1141: H.-M. Voigt, W. Ebeling, I. Rechenberg, H.-P. Schwefel (Eds.), Parallel Problem Solving from Nature – PPSN IV. Proceedings, 1996. XVII, 1.050 pages. 1996.

Vol. 1142: R.W. Hartenstein, M. Glesner (Eds.), Field-Programmable Logic. Proceedings, 1996. X, 432 pages. 1996.

Vol. 1143: T.C. Fogarty (Ed.), Evolutionary Computing. Proceedings, 1996. VIII, 305 pages. 1996.

Vol. 1144: J. Ponce, A. Zisserman, M. Hebert (Eds.), Object Representation in Computer Vision. Proceedings, 1996. VIII, 403 pages. 1996.

Vol. 1145: R. Cousot, D.A. Schmidt (Eds.), Static Analysis. Proceedings, 1996. IX, 389 pages. 1996.

Vol. 1146: E. Bertino, H. Kurth, G. Martella, E. Montolivo (Eds.), Computer Security – ESORICS 96. Proceedings, 1996. X, 365 pages. 1996.

Vol. 1147: L. Miclet, C. de la Higuera (Eds.), Grammatical Inference: Learning Syntax from Sentences. Proceedings, 1996. VIII, 327 pages. 1996. (Subseries LNAI).

Vol. 1148: M.C. Lin, D. Manocha (Eds.), Applied Computational Geometry. Proceedings, 1996. VIII, 223 pages. 1996.

Vol. 1149: C. Montangero (Ed.), Software Process Technology. Proceedings, 1996. IX, 291 pages. 1996.

Vol. 1150: A. Hlawiczka, J.G. Silva, L. Simoncini (Eds.), Dependable Computing – EDCC-2. Proceedings, 1996. XVI, 440 pages. 1996.

Vol. 1151: Ö. Babaoğlu, K. Marzullo (Eds.), Distributed Algorithms. Proceedings, 1996. VIII, 381 pages. 1996.

Vol. 1152: T. Furuhashi, Y. Uchikawa (Eds.), Fuzzy Logic, Neural Networks, and Evolutionary Computation. Proceedings, 1995. VIII, 243 pages. 1996. (Subseries LNAI).

Vol. 1153: E. Burke, P. Ross (Eds.), Practice and Theory of Automated Timetabling. Proceedings, 1995. XIII, 381 pages. 1996.

Vol. 1154: D. Pedreschi, C. Zaniolo (Eds.), Logic in Databases. Proceedings, 1996. X, 497 pages. 1996.

Vol. 1155: J. Roberts, U. Mocci, J. Virtamo (Eds.), Broadbank Network Teletraffic. XXII, 584 pages. 1996.

Vol. 1156: A. Bode, J. Dongarra, T. Ludwig, V. Sunderam (Eds.), Parallel Virtual Machine – EuroPVM '96. Proceedings, 1996. XIV, 362 pages. 1996.

Vol. 1157: B. Thalheim (Ed.), Conceptual Modeling – ER '96. Proceedings, 1996. XII, 489 pages. 1996.

Vol. 1158: S. Berardi, M. Coppo (Eds.), Types for Proofs and Programs. Proceedings, 1995. X, 296 pages. 1996.

Vol. 1159: D.L. Borges, C.A.A. Kaestner (Eds.), Advances in Artificial Intelligence. Proceedings, 1996. XI, 243 pages. (Subseries LNAI).

Vol. 1160: S. Arikawa, A.K. Sharma (Eds.), Algorithmic Learning Theory. Proceedings, 1996. XVII, 337 pages. 1996. (Subseries LNAI).

Vol. 1161: O. Spaniol, C. Linnhoff-Popien, B. Meyer (Eds.), Trends in Distributed Systems. Proceedings, 1996. VIII, 289 pages. 1996.

Vol. 1162: D.G. Feitelson, L. Rudolph (Eds.), Job Scheduling Strategies for Parallel Processing. Proceedings, 1996. VIII, 291 pages. 1996.

Vol. 1163: K. Kim, T. Matsumoto (Eds.), Advances in Cryptology – ASIACRYPT '96. Proceedings, 1996. XII, 395 pages. 1996.

Vol. 1164: K. Berquist, A. Berquist (Eds.), Managing Information Highways. XIV, 417 pages. 1996.

Vol. 1165: J.-R. Abrial, E. Börger, H. Langmaack (Eds.), Formal Methods for Industrial Applications. VIII, 511 pages. 1996.

Vol. 1166: M. Srivas, A. Camilleri (Eds.), Formal Methods in Computer-Aided Design. Proceedings, 1996. IX, 470 pages. 1996.

Vol. 1167: I. Sommerville (Ed.), Software Configuration Management. VII, 291 pages. 1996.

Vol. 1168: I. Smith, B. Faltings (Eds.), Advances in Case-Based Reasoning. Proceedings, 1996. IX, 531 pages. 1996. (Subseries LNAI).

Vol. 1169: M. Broy, S. Merz, K. Spies (Eds.), Formal Systems Specification. XXIII, 541 pages. 1996.

Vol. 1170: M. Nagl (Ed.), Building Tightly Integrated Software Development Environments: The IPSEN Approach. IX, 709 pages. 1996.

Vol. 1171: A. Franz, Automatic Ambiguity Resolution in Natural Language Processing. XIX, 155 pages. 1996. (Subseries LNAI).

Vol. 1172: J. Pieprzyk, J. Seberry (Eds.), Information Security and Privacy. Proceedings, 1996. IX, 333 pages. 1996.

Vol. 1173: W. Rucklidge, Efficient Visual Recognition Using the Hausdorff Distance. XIII, 178 pages. 1996.

Vol. 1174: R. Anderson (Ed.), Information Hiding. Proceedings, 1996. VIII, 351 pages. 1996.

Vol. 1175: K.G. Jeffery, J. Král, M. Bartošek (Eds.), SOFSEM'96: Theory and Practice of Informatics. Proceedings, 1996. XII, 491 pages. 1996.

Vol. 1176: S. Miguet, A. Montanvert, S. Ubéda (Eds.), Discrete Geometry for Computer Imagery. Proceedings, 1996. XI, 349 pages. 1996.

Vol. 1177: J.P. Müller, The Design of Intelligent Agents. XV, 227 pages. 1996. (Subseries LNAI).

Vol. 1178: T. Asano, Y. Igarashi, H. Nagamochi, S. Miyano, S. Suri (Eds.), Algorithms and Computation. Proceedings, 1996. X, 448 pages. 1996.

Vol. 1179: J. Jaffar, R.H.C. Yap (Eds.), Concurrency and Parallelism, Programming, Networking, and Security. Proceedings, 1996. XIII, 394 pages. 1996.

Vol. 1180: V. Chandru, V. Vinay (Eds.), Foundations of Software Technology and Theoretical Computer Science. Proceedings, 1996. XI, 387 pages. 1996.

Vol. 1181: D. Bjørner, M. Broy, I.V. Pottosin (Eds.), Perspectives of System Informatics. Proceedings, 1996. XVII, 447 pages. 1996.

Vol. 1182: W. Hasan, Optimization of SQL Queries for Parallel Machines. XVIII, 133 pages. 1996.

Vol. 1183: A. Wierse, G.G. Grinstein, U. Lang (Eds.), Database Issues for Data Visualization. Proceedings, 1995. XIV, 219 pages. 1996.

Vol. 1184: J. Waśniewski, J. Dongarra, K. Madsen, D. Olesen (Eds.), Applied Parallel Computing. Proceedings, 1996. XIII, 722 pages. 1996.

Vol. 1185: G. Ventre, J. Domingo-Pascual, A. Danthine (Eds.), Multimedia Telecommunications and Applications. Proceedings, 1996. XII, 267 pages. 1996.

Vol. 1186: F. Afrati, P. Kolaitis (Eds.), Database Theory - ICDT'97. Proceedings, 1997. XIII, 477 pages. 1997.